MONASTERY GUEST HOUSES
OF NORTH AMERICA

MONASTERY GUEST HOUSES
OF NORTH AMERICA

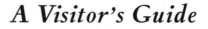

A Visitor's Guide

5TH EDITION

Robert J. Regalbuto

THE COUNTRYMAN PRESS
WOODSTOCK, VERMONT

ACKNOWLEDGMENTS

I am grateful to the nuns, monks, and others who have graciously provided hospitality to me. I also extend a special word of gratitude to the monastics and guest house administrators without whose cooperation and information this book would not have been possible. Thanks also to Kermit Hummel, Lisa Sacks, and Melissa Dobson of The Countryman Press.

ISBN 978-0-88150-900-7

CIP data are available.

Cover photo: The setting sun brings vespers at St. Benedict's Monastery. Used with the kind permission of John Ruzicka and St. Benedict's Monastery, Snowmass, Colorado, © John Ruzicka and St. Benedict's Monastery.

Book design and composition by Susan Livingston
Artwork by Jennifer Bailey appears on pages 1, 5, 21, 35, 37, 59, 61, 65, 81, 91, 99, 101, 103, 105, 113, 115, 117, 121, 129, 135, 139, 153, 159, 167, 175, 177, 181, 197, 203, 205, 207, 209, 211, 215, 231, 235, 241, and 251.
Artwork by B. Griffiths appears on pages 13, 23, 27, 39, 47, 49, 55, 69, 73, 79, 85, 93, 97, 107, 123, 125, 137, 141, 145, 147, 151, 171, 187, 195, 201, 223, 227, 233, 245, and 257.

Published by The Countryman Press,
P.O. Box 748, Woodstock, VT 05091
Distributed by W. W. Norton & Company, Inc.,
500 Fifth Avenue, New York, NY 10110
Printed in the United States of America

10 9 8 7 6 5 4 3 2 1

CONTENTS

CONNECTICUT

DISTRICT OF COLUMBIA

FLORIDA

GEORGIA

IDAHO

ILLINOIS

INDIANA

IOWA

KANSAS

KENTUCKY

LOUISIANA

MAINE

MARYLAND

MASSACHUSETTS

MICHIGAN

MINNESOTA

MISSISSIPPI

MISSOURI

OREGON

PENNSYLVANIA

RHODE ISLAND

SOUTH CAROLINA

TENNESSEE

TEXAS

UTAH

VERMONT

VIRGINIA

WASHINGTON

WISCONSIN

❖ CANADA

PREFACE

Let all guests that come be received like Christ Himself, for
He will say: "I was a stranger and ye took me in." . . .
Let the care of the guest house, also, be entrusted to a
brother whose soul is possessed with the fear of God: let
there be sufficient beds prepared there and let the house of
God be wisely governed by prudent men.

Saint Benedict wrote these words in his Holy Rule for monks in sixth-century Italy. In this spirit many monasteries open their guest houses to modern-day pilgrims seeking a time of quiet, rest, refreshment, and renewal. As the *National Catholic Reporter* stated, "Here is an alternative for people who like vacations that heal, are truly restful and economical."

I have been lodging in monastery guest houses for 45 years, and I wrote my first guide to monastery guest houses 20 years ago. This book is based on my travels and research. The information here is not only current but also comprehensive, including guest houses in urban and rural locales from coast to coast, and featuring accommodations offered by communities of several denominations: Roman Catholic, Anglican/Episcopal, Eastern Orthodox, Lutheran, Quaker, Presbyterian, Methodist, Congregationalist, Unitarian Universalist, and ecumenical. So, too, the monasteries, convents, and other places listed represent a spectrum of traditions and observances: some traditional, some contemporary, and others *via media*. Each of these extends hospitality to those of other faiths—or no faith.

An excellent approach for the newcomer at a monastery guest house is to remember that a religious community is a family, and that, like every family, it has its own traditions, customs, and rules. But no need to worry—monasteries are used to newcomers and guests. The guest master or guest mistress, other community members, and/or guest literature will help familiarize you with house rules so that you can settle in comfortably and enjoy your stay.

Some practical advice:

• Reservations should be made as far in advance as possible. Some monastery guest houses are so popular that booking well in advance is not only advisable but necessary.

• If you wish to lodge in a monastery guest house but not participate in a group retreat program, make this known at the time you make a reservation, stating that you would like a "private retreat."

• Charges quoted here are current at the time of writing but subject to change. (Canadian charges are given in Canadian dollars.)

• Be prepared to make payment with cash or a check. It is rare that credit or debit cards are accepted, but this is not unheard of. Be sure to inquire about payment methods before your stay.

• Rooms are typically clean, comfortable, and simply furnished. Do not expect modern amenities in guest rooms such as a telephone, radio, television, or computer. If you bring a listening device, be sure it has ear buds.

It is my hope that this guide will lead you, the reader, to a "place apart," where monastic hospitality is offered and a "holy leisure" is enjoyed.

He saith unto them,
Come and see.

—JOHN 1:39

UNITED STATES

✦ ALABAMA

Sacred Heart Monastery
Benedictine Sisters Retreat Center

916 Convent Rd. NE, Cullman, AL 35055-2019

Order: Benedictine Sisters (Roman Catholic)

Contact: Office Manager

Telephone: 256-734-8302. **Best time to call:** Mon. to Fri., 9 AM to 4 PM Central Time

Web site: www.shmon.org; **e-mail:** retreats@shmon.org

Accommodations: Houses up to 69 guests in single, twin-bedded, and triple-bedded rooms, most with shared baths

Meals: Three meals daily

Costs: $75 per person for first night; $50 each subsequent night, meals included. Contact office manager for group rates.

Directions: From Birmingham take I-65 North to Exit 308 and continue east on US 278. At Convent Rd. turn left at three-way traffic light. Enter second gate on right.

Public Transportation: Contact office manager for information.

History: There has been a Benedictine presence in Alabama since the 1860s, when monks came here from Pennsylvania. Later in the 19th century Benedictine sisters arrived and opened Sacred Heart Monastery. At the turn of the 20th century the large and impressive Gothic Revival monastery and chapel were built.

Description: Guests may explore the monastery's 200-acre property. Nearby is St. Bernard Abbey, which is home to 40 monks. St. Bernard Abbey Church and Sacred Heart Chapel are a study in contrasts in terms of architectural style. Sacred Heart was built in traditional medieval Gothic style with authentic details, while the church at St. Bernard is a more modified and modern interpretation of the same architectural principles.

Point of Interest: While visiting St. Bernard Abbey, be sure to see the Ave Maria Grotto. The lifetime work of a monk who undertook the project in the 1930s, the Grotto is one of the most popular tourist attractions in Alabama, a major link in the Bible Belt.

Special Note: Reservations are required for the Benedictine Sisters Retreat Center, which publishes a full schedule of programs, available on request and posted on the monastery's Web site.

Visitation Monastery
Sacred Heart Retreat House

2300 Spring Hill Ave., Mobile, AL 36607

Order: Visitation Sisters (Roman Catholic)

Contact: Guest Sister

Telephone: 251-473-2321. **Best time to call:** 9 AM to 7 PM Central Time

Web site: www.visitationmonasterymobile.org

Accommodations: Houses up to 44 guests in single rooms; two rooms have private baths.

Meals: Guests provide their own food; a refrigerator, microwave oven, and sink are available. Catering service can be arranged for groups.

Costs: $50 per person per day for room only. "A voluntary offering or flat group rate can be considered."

Directions: The monastery's Web site includes a map. For further directions by car or by public transportation, contact the guest sister.

History: In 1832 five sisters from Georgetown Visitation Monastery in Washington, D.C., boarded a ship and sailed toward Mobile to start a new monastery. After a month's journey they arrived in Alabama and founded the monastery and a school, both of which were completed in 1855. About a century later the school was closed and the building became Sacred Heart Retreat House. In 1957 the sisters opened a candy kitchen, where they continue to produce Heavenly Hash and other confections. The chapel, built in 1895, was restored in 1999.

Description: The monastery and chapel have been designated a historic site by the Historic Mobile Preservation Society and are featured in the Historic American Buildings Survey, a project of the Library of Congress. The antebellum guest house has wrought-iron balconies overlooking a tree-shaded garden and gazebo. The former chaplain's residence is now a book and gift shop where the nuns' candies are sold.

Points of Interest: Mobile is home to colleges, historic buildings and churches, museums, lush gardens, and pristine beaches.

Special Note: "Since we are a monastic community, it is not possible for us to have guests arriving after 8 PM."

✤ ALASKA

The Shrine of St. Therese Lodge and Cabins
5933 Lund St., Juneau, AK 99801

Order: Founded by Jesuits (Roman Catholic)

Contact: Director

Telephone: 907-780-6112. **Best time to call:** 8 AM to 5 PM Alaska Time

Web site: www.shrineofsainttherese.org; **e-mail:** juneaushrine@gci.net

Accommodations: The lodge accommodates groups of up to 22 guests in ten rooms, all with shared baths. Two new structures, the Jubilee Cabin and the Little Flower Retreat, overlook the Inner Passage waters of the Pacific Ocean. In addition, there are two log cabins for individuals, couples, families, or small-group retreats: one with a kitchenette and private bath, the other being quite small, with a wood-burning stove.

Meals: Contact director

Costs: Rates are variable; contact director

Directions: From Juneau take AK 7 (Eagan Dr.) Northwest. This becomes the Glacier Highway. At Mile 22.5 look for sign on right, directing you to turn left on gravel road ahead; this road leads to shrine.

Public Transportation: There is air and ferry service to Juneau, where you can rent a car or take a taxi to the shrine (23 miles).

History: A Jesuit priest, Father William LeVasseur, was inspired to build the shrine in the 1930s, and received the blessing of Bishop Joseph Crimont, also a Jesuit, for its foundation. Father LeVasseur's dream became a reality when he celebrated the inaugural mass in the shrine's chapel in 1941.

Description: The shrine is on 46 acres. This includes the stone chapel, which is on an island accessible by path over a causeway. Two of Alaska's bishops are interred in the chapel crypt. There are also trails, gardens, a labyrinth, the Stations of the Cross, and a columbarium. Everywhere, one is surrounded by nature's beauty, and it is not unusual to see salmon, whales, sea lions, soaring eagles, and other creatures here.

Points of Interest: A place of stunning natural beauty, Alaska has glaciers and other spectacular sights.

> *The sea is his and he made it; and his hands*
> *prepared the dry land.*
>
> —PSALM 95

❖ ARIZONA

Holy Trinity Monastery

P.O. Box 298, St. David, AZ 85630

Order: Benedictine Monks (Roman Catholic)

Contact: Guest Master

Telephone: 520-720-4016 or 520-720-4642. **Best time to call:** Mon. to Sat. 9 AM to 4 PM Mountain Time

Web site: www.holytrinitymonastery.org; **e-mail:** guestmaster@theriver.com

Accommodations: Guest house accommodates up to 48 people in single and twin-bedded rooms, some with private baths

Meals: Three meals daily

Costs: $50 per person per day for room and meals

Directions: From Tucson, take I-10 East to AZ 80 to town of St. David. The monastery is south of St. David between mileposts 302 and 303.

Public Transportation: There is air service to Tucson, and Greyhound bus and Amtrak train service to Benson (9 miles from the monastery). Contact the guest master for further information.

History: In 1974 the Roman Catholic bishop of Tucson invited Benedictine monks to establish a Christian renewal center in this, Cochise County. The invitation was accepted by Father Louis B. Hasenfuss and two postulants of the Benedictine Abbey in Pecos, New Mexico. Within two months of their arrival, ground was broken for Our Lady of Guadalupe Church.

Description: The church is inspired by the pueblo style so prevalent in the American Southwest. Both church and monastery are sited on 148 acres bordered by a bird sanctuary trail. Holy Trinity Monastery (often abbreviated HTM) has an oriental garden, Gallery Trinitas (a museum and art gallery), a bookstore and gift shop, a thrift shop, and an RV park. The Whetstone Mountains form a breathtaking backdrop to the west.

Special Note: Holy Trinity is unique in that this is a residential community of monks, sisters, and laity who live the Benedictine Rule. Further, HTM has more than 400 oblates (associates) across the United States and abroad. The monastery is ecumenical in its outreach.

Santa Rita Abbey

HC1 Box 929, 42000 Fish Canyon Rd., Sonoita, AZ 85637

Order: Cistercian (Trappistine) Nuns (Roman Catholic)

Contact: Guest Mistress

Telephone: 520-455-5595. **Best time to call:** 8:30 AM to 11 AM and 2 PM to 4 PM Mountain Time

Web site: www.santaritaabbey.org; **e-mail:** sracommty@wildblue.net

Accommodations: Guest house accommodates eight persons in six single rooms and one twin-bedded room, each with private bath.

Meals: "Simple-to-prepare foods are provided"; guests prepare their own meals.

Costs: $35 per person per night, including food

Directions: From Tucson take I-10 East to Exit 281, then follow AZ 83 (Sonoita/Patagonia) for 21 miles, taking a right on Garner Canyon Rd. After 1 mile, turn right on Fish Canyon Rd. Continue 1 mile and bear left at fork in road toward abbey. Guests are asked to check in at monastery.

Public Transportation: Contact the guest mistress for information.

History: "Our community of nine sisters has been here since 1972, the foundress coming from our monastery in Wrentham, Massachusetts. Ours is a very old monastic order, a life of prayer, work to support ourselves (making altar breads), study, and community life. A quiet life at the service of God's people."

Description: Santa Rita Abbey is located in the desert foothills of the Santa Rita Mountains.

Points of Interest: Mount Wrightson, the historic town of Patagonia, and bird sanctuaries are nearby.

Special Note: Guests are asked to arrive before 7 PM.

> *And he saith unto them, Come ye yourselves apart into a desert place, and rest awhile . . ."*
>
> —MARK 6:31

Servants of Christ Priory

28 W. Pasadena Ave., Phoenix, AZ 85013-2002

Order: Benedictine Monks (Episcopal)

Contact: Guest Master

Telephone: 602-248-9321

E-mail: cderijk@earthlink.net

Accommodations: Priory accommodates five guests in single and twin rooms, two of which have private bath.

Meals: One meal daily

Costs: $80 per day for room and meal

Directions: From Phoenix, take I-17 to Camelback Rd. exit going east. At Third Ave., turn left and go one block, turning right on W. Pasadena Ave. Priory is on left.

From I-10, take the AZ 51 turnoff to Highland Ave. Turn left at light and go one block to 16th St. Go one block on 16th St. to Camelback Rd. and turn left onto Central Ave. Go one block on Central and turn right onto W. Pasadena Ave.

Public Transportation: The SuperShuttle van service will take you from Phoenix Sky Harbor International Airport to the priory door. There is also bus service and Amtrak passenger rail service to Phoenix. Contact guest master for further information.

History: Founded in 1968 as a community of priests and laymen, the apostolate of the Servants of Christ Priory is to be a monastic witness in an urban environment. The current priory property was acquired in 1989.

Description: The priory offers a place of silence and refuge within the city of Phoenix. An attractive brick building, the priory is surrounded by trees, and potted plants greet the visitor at the front door. The Chapel of the Transfiguration and the adjoining guest house are set back at the far end of the property. There is also a bookstore where prayer books, hymnals, Bibles, icons, religious jewelry, candles, altar bread, inspirational books, CDs, and greeting cards are sold.

Points of Interest: Of particular interest to guests may be the Prayer Garden in Phoenix. It is maintained and opened to the public by the Evangelical Sisterhood of Mary. The Sisterhood is a Lutheran community founded in Germany following World War II.

Phoenix is the capital of Arizona. The city has a number of museums, the Heard Museum being most noted for its collections devoted to Arizona's history, Indian culture, anthropology, and art. The Desert Botanical Garden, Encanto Park, Pueblo Grande Museum and Archaeological Park, and South Mountain Park are also nearby. The city of Scottsdale is adjacent to Phoenix. Sedona, Montezuma Castle National Monument, and the Grand Canyon National Park are north of the city and priory.

> *Praise, O ye servants of the Lord,*
> *Praise the name of the Lord.*

> —PSALM 113

✤ ARKANSAS

Subiaco Abbey
Coury House Retreat Center

405 N. Subiaco Ave., Subiaco, AR 72865

Order: Benedictine Monks (Roman Catholic)

Contact: Secretary

Telephone: 479-934-4411

Web site: www.subi.org; **e-mail:** couryhouse@subi.org

Accommodations: Coury House accommodates up to 73 guests in 29 twin-bedded rooms, five double-bedded rooms, one queen-bedded room, and a handicap-accessible suite for up to three people. Each room has its own private bathroom with shower.

Meals: Three meals daily

Costs: Room rates per night are $40 for single occupancy, $50 for double occupancy, and $60 for triple occupancy. Meal costs are $6 for breakfast, $6 for lunch, and $8 for dinner.

Directions: Subiaco Abbey is located 125 miles west of Little Rock. Take I-40 West to Exit 55, then follow the signs for abbey. From Fort Smith, take AR 22 for 48 miles east to Subiaco.

Public Transportation: Fort Smith Regional Airport is recommended. Contact the secretary for additional information.

History: Saint Benedict established a monastery at Subiaco, Italy, in the sixth century. Some 1,300 years later, an American Subiaco Abbey was founded in 1878 by monks from St. Meinrad's Abbey, Indiana, to minister to the German immigrant population in western Arkansas and Texas. The monks of Subiaco established parishes, schools, and, in 1963, Coury House—a guest and retreat center to offer a quiet place for prayer, reflection, and spiritual direction for those seeking "a place apart."

Description: The abbey church, modified Romanesque in style, was completed in 1959. Of special note are the 182 German stained-glass windows depicting episodes in the life of Saint Benedict. The church, bell tower, and cloister are all constructed of native sandstone. Spacious and well-manicured grounds surround the abbey. Here, one may explore the walking and hiking paths, meditative areas, a grotto, beautiful gazebos, and out-of-doors Stations of the Cross, which, at the time of writing, were being restored.

Points of Interest: Majestic Mount Magazine is 20 miles south of Subiaco. The Post and Wiederkehr wineries, and historic St. Mary's Catholic Church in Altus, are 35 miles from the abbey.

✤ CALIFORNIA

Abbey of New Clairvaux

P.O. Box 80, Vina, CA 96092

Order: Cistercian (Trappist) Monks (Roman Catholic)

Contact: Guest Master

Telephone: 530-839-2434

Web site: www.newclairvaux.org; **e-mail:** reservation@newclairvaux.org

Accommodations: Guests house accommodates 10 guests in six single rooms and two twin-bedded suites, all with private baths.

Meals: Three meals daily

Costs: Requested donation of $60 per person per night for room and meals

Directions: The abbey is north of San Francisco and Sacramento, between Chico and Redbluff off either I-5 (take South Ave. East) or CA 99 (turn left at the Woodson Bridge turnoff).

Public Transportation: With prior notice, monks will provide transportation to and from Greyhound bus station or airport in Chico (about 30 minutes away) and bus station in Corning (about 15 minutes away). Contact guest master for further information.

History: The monastery takes its name from the Abbey of Clairvaux in France, founded by the Cistercian Saint Bernard in 1115. Clairvaux may be translated as "clear valley," or "valley of light." In the early 1950s monks from Gethsemani Abbey, Kentucky, visited California to search for a site for a new monastery. They acquired Vina Ranch, which had been a winery and dairy farm once owned by Leland Stanford, the namesake of Stanford University. Though the Stanford mansion perished in a blaze in 1970, other buildings remain, including the winery, whiskey barn, red barn, tailor shop, novitiate house, St. Luke's Dining Room, and St. Matthew and St. John's guest houses. In the 1980s the guest facilities were improved with the building of a welcoming center, two new guest houses, a guest chapel, and library. The most recent and significant addition to the abbey is the Santa Maria de Ovila Chapter House. Built for a Cistercian abbey in Spain in the 13th century, the chapter house was moved, stone by stone, from Spain to New Spain (California). This was financed by William Randolph Hearst in 1931 to house a museum. The museum was never built and the stones remained in a heap until 2001, when they were given to the abbey. Now reconstructed, the Ovila Chapter House is open for visitors to tour.

Description: New Clairvaux Abbey has 590 acres. Here the monks cultivate prunes, walnuts, cereal crops, and grapevines for their livelihood. There are a winery and tasting room at 26240 7th Street in Vina.

The ninth degree of humility is, that a monk refrain his tongue from speaking, keeping silence until a question is asked him, as the Scripture sheweth: "In much talking thou shalt not avoid sin": and "The talkative man shall not be directed upon the earth."

—RULE OF SAINT BENEDICT

Incarnation Monastery

1369 La Loma Ave., Berkeley, CA 94708

Order: Camaldolese Benedictine Monks (Roman Catholic)

Contact: Father Arthur Poulin, Er. Cam., Guest Master

Telephone: 510-845-0601. Best times to call: 9 AM to 12 noon or 4 PM to 5 PM Pacific Time

Web site: www.contemplation.com/hermitage/incarnation.html

Accommodations: Monastery houses up to five guests in four single rooms and one room with queen-sized bed, all with shared baths.

Meals: No meals are provided. However, there is a small kitchenette and you may "bring your own provisions."

Costs: Suggested donation of $50 per person per day

Directions: From I-80 North, make right turn onto University Ave., left turn onto Oxford St., and right turn onto Cedar St. La Loma Ave. will be on left.

Public Transportation: Take BART (Bay Area Rapid Transit) subway to Downtown Berkeley Station.

History: Two men have had key roles in the history of the Camaldolese. The first was Saint Benedict. He lived in sixth-century Italy and is known as the father of Western monasticism and the founder of the Benedictine Order. The second was Saint Romuald, who in the 11th century revitalized a part of the Benedictine Order at Camaldoli, Italy, infusing it with a vocation expressed in two lifestyles: that lived in a community and that of a hermit in solitude. In 1958 the Camaldolese arrived in the U.S. and established a monastery at Big Sur, California. Incarnation Monastery, their house of studies, was opened in the 1990s.

Description: The monastery has a beautiful view of the northern part of San Francisco Bay, and adjoining it is a very pleasant public park. The main campus of the University of California at Berkeley is just a few blocks from the monastery, and the Graduate Theological Union is close by. The GTU combines nine seminaries (Episcopal, Baptist, Lutheran, Presbyterian,

Unitarian, Interdenominational, and three Roman Catholic). Orthodox, Judaic, and Buddhist institutes are also in the area.

Points of Interest: Berkeley and the Bay Area offer numerous opportunities for cultural expression in the arts, music, and dance. As the monks at Incarnation Monastery suggest, "Why not re-create yourself with a cultural retreat linked to the prayer and hospitality of the monastery?"

Monastery of St. John of San Francisco

P.O. Box 439, 21770 Ponderosa Way, Manton, CA 96059

Order: Monks (Orthodox Church in America)

Contact: Guest Master

Telephone: 530-474-5964 or 530-474-3405. **Best time to call:** Tues. to Sat. 10 AM to 4 PM Pacific Time, or leave a message anytime

Web site: www.monasteryofstjohn.org; **e-mail:** office@monasteryof stjohn.org

Accommodations: Guest house accommodates up to 19 guests in four rooms, one of which has a double bed. Three other rooms each have four beds. There are two shared baths.

Meals: "The monks provide one formal meal on weekdays around midday. The morning and evening meals are informal (buffet). On the weekends there is a formal brunch and formal supper. Formal meals are served and are accompanied by spiritual readings. Informal meals are taken in relative silence. The guest house has a small kitchen, although guests are welcome to join the monks for all their meals."

Costs: "There are no fees for staying with us, but if you are able, we have a suggested donation to help us offset costs." Suggested donation is $40 per person per day for room and meals, $60 per couple per day, and $75 per family per day.

Directions: *Note:* The monks have advised that GPS and online map/direction sources are inaccurate for this location. From points south take I-5 to CA 36 East in Red Bluff. Drive 14 miles to Manton Rd. (County Route A6). Turn left on Manton Rd. (note sign to Manton) and drive another 14 miles. Turn right at the Manton store onto Forward Rd. and drive 3.8 miles. Then turn left on Ponderosa Way. Monastery is on right.

From points north, take I-5 South to CA 44 East in Redding. Drive to Shingletown. Turn right at library at Wilson Hill Rd. Follow signs to Manton (about 8.1 miles). Go straight onto Forward Rd. Continue another 3.8 miles, then turn left on Ponderosa Way. Monastery is on right.

Public Transportation: There is Greyhound bus service to Redding and to Red Bluff. Contact guest master in advance to be met at bus station.

History: The monastery was founded in 1996 under the leadership of then Hieromonk Jonah, who has since become the head of the Orthodox Church in America. Originally in Point Reyes Station, California, the Brotherhood moved to Manton in 2006. There are now 16 monks in residence. Here they "seek to live the traditional Orthodox monastic life as established by St. Pachomios and St. Basil in the fourth century and as guided by the teachings and examples of subsequent Holy Fathers. We are informed and inspired by the living tradition of the ancient monastic centers, including Mt. Athos in Greece, and Valaam in Russia. Along with these two monastic centers, we worship according to the Julian or 'old' calendar, which is currently 13 days behind the civil calendar . . . We struggle to be faithful to holy tradition while adapting to the realities of contemporary America. We are a multi-national community and [our] services are in English . . . We strive to earn our living by candle making, publishing, woodworking, and operating a bookstore. We also grow some of our own food and raise poultry for eggs and goats for milk."

Description: The monastery owns 42 acres of scenic ponderosa forest in the foothills of the Cascade Mountains. The guest house has a common room with a fireplace.

Point of Interest: Lassen Volcanic National Park is nearby.

Let us who mystically represent the Cherubim
and sing the Thrice-Holy Hymn to the life-giving Trinity,
put away all worldly care.
　　　—DIVINE LITURGY OF SAINT JOHN CHRYSOSTOM

Mount Tabor Monastery

P.O. Box 217, Redwood Valley, CA 95470-0217

Order: The Monks of Mount Tabor (Ukrainian Catholic)

Contact: Brother Andrew, Guest Master

Telephone: 707-485-8959 (Leave message on answering machine)

Web site: www.byzcath.org/monastery

Accommodations: Retreat house accommodates up to 19 guests in ten single rooms, one twin-bedded room, and two dormitories with bunk beds. All have shared baths.

Meals: Three meals daily (according to monastic diet and fastings)

Costs: $40 per person per day for room and meals; $50 per day for married couples

Directions: From US 101, just north of CA 20 (about 7 miles north of Ukiah), take West Rd. exit and turn right off ramp. In 3.3 miles road ends at T intersection; turn left onto Tomki Rd. Monastery will be on right, about 1mile after road ascends hill.

Public Transportation: From San Francisco International Airport, take Santa Rosa Airporter bus to Sonoma County Airport, and from there take MTA bus to Ukiah, where a pickup can be arranged.

History: Mount Tabor Monastery was founded in the early 1970s by Archimandrite Boniface Luykx, who was widely known as a theologian, academic, liturgist, and an expert on Eastern Christian spirituality.

Description: Mount Tabor includes 240 heavily wooded hillside acres. The monastery and church, designed in traditional Ukrainian architectural style, are built of timber and crowned with domes and crosses. Each of the half dozen monks in residence lives in an individual 10-by-12-foot house. The retreat house is apart from the village of monks and farther up the hill. Guests may wish to explore the main trail, which continues past the retreat house to the hill's summit.

Point of Interest: The nearby Redwood Forest State Park features some of the world's tallest trees.

New Camaldoli Hermitage

62475 Highway 1, Big Sur, CA 93920

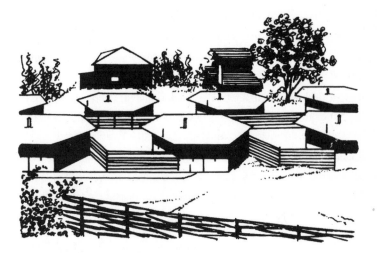

Order: Camaldolese Benedictine Monks (Roman Catholic)

Contact: Guest Master

Telephone: 831-667-2456

Web site: www.contemplation.com/Hermitage/retreat.html

Accommodations: Monastery and retreat house accommodate up to nine guests, each in a single room with a toilet and washbasin. Showers are shared. In addition, there are five trailer-hermitages on the property; each can accommodate one guest.

Meals: Three vegetarian meals daily

Costs: $70 per person per day for room and meals in the retreat house; $80 per person per day in trailer-hermitage

Directions: The hermitage is located at Lucia, off the Pacific Coast Highway (CA 1), about 25 miles south of Big Sur and 55 miles south of Monterey. The hermitage entrance road, on the inland side of the highway, is marked by a large wooden cross.

Public Transportation: There is air and bus service to Monterey, where guests may be met by a monk (with prior arrangement) on Fri. evenings between 5 PM and 7 PM.

History: The Camaldolese hermits were founded by Saint Romuald at Camaldoli, Italy, in 1012. They are a reform within the Order of St. Benedict. The hermits may lead either a solitary life or a life in community. New Camaldoli opened at Big Sur in 1958.

Description: New Camaldoli Hermitage is on a 500-acre tract of land in the Santa Lucia mountain range. Guests will find every opportunity for solitude here. The guest rooms have views of the Pacific Ocean.

Special Note: Preached retreats are given five or six times a year. The schedule for the following calendar year is published every fall. Literature and further information are available from the hermitage's guest master.

It is well known that there are four kinds of monks. The first are the cenobites: that is those in monasteries, who live under a rule or an abbot. The second are the anchorites or hermits . . .

—RULE OF SAINT BENEDICT

Prince of Peace Abbey

650 Benet Hill Rd., Oceanside, CA 92058-1253

Order: Benedictine Monks (Roman Catholic)

Contact: Guest Master

Telephone: 760-967-4200, ext. 248

Web site: www.princeofpeaceabbey.org; **e-mail:** abbeyretreat@aol.com

Accommodations: Retreat house accommodates up to 44 guests, in single and double rooms, each with private bath.

Meals: Three meals daily

Costs: $85 per person per night for room and meals

Directions: From I-5 North to Oceanside, exit onto CA 76 East. Turn left on Benet Rd. This will take you over a two-lane bridge. Turn left (west) on Airport Rd.; travel less than 0.5 mile. Turn right at second driveway and drive to top of hill.

From I-15 (traveling north or south), exit at CA 76. Travel west on 76 about 17 miles through town of Bonsall and continue on to Oceanside. Exit right on Benet Rd. Continue as above.

Public Transportation: There is bus and Amtrak service to Oceanside. Contact the guest master for further information.

History: Prince of Peace Abbey was founded in 1958 by monks from St. Meinrad Archabbey in Indiana.

Description: The abbey, its monastery, church, and retreat house are located about 100 miles south of Los Angeles and 35 miles north of San Diego. The abbey is built on a mesa overlooking the San Luis Rey River Valley and the Pacific Ocean.

Point of Interest: The abbey is a short distance from the historic Mission San Luis Rey de Francia, which dates to 1798.

St. Andrew's Abbey

P.O. Box 40, 31001 N. Valyermo Rd., Valyermo, CA 93563

Order: Benedictine Monks (Roman Catholic)

Contact: Guest Master

Telephone: 661-944-2178

Web site: www.valyermo.com; **e-mail:** monks@valyermo.com

Accommodations: Guest house accommodates up to 34 persons in 17 twin-bedded rooms, each with private bath

Meals: Three meals daily

Costs: Recommended donation of $70 per person per day for room and meals, single occupancy, $60 per person in a shared room. For a three-day weekend (Fri. to Sun.) price is $225 per person, single occupancy, and $150 per person, double occupancy. "We do have a limited number of partial scholarships thanks to the generosity of those who are able to give more money than the recommended donation. We hope others who are able will also contribute so that we may offer hospitality to all who need our assistance."

Directions: From Los Angeles, take CA 14 North to Pearblossom Highway exit. Go up to Longview Rd. and then turn left on Avenue W, which becomes Valyermo Rd.

Public Transportation: There is Greyhound bus service to Palmdale, and Metrolink commuter rail service to Acton. Contact guest master for further information.

History: St. Andrew's Abbey traces its roots to the Belgian Abbey of Saint Andrew. Belgian monks were sent to China in 1929, and when the Benedictines were expelled by the Communists in 1952, the monks came to the U.S., settling in Valyermo in 1955. From the beginning, monastic hospitality has been a work of the monks here, and in 1958 a guest house was opened. The Welcome Center has a shop (Abbey Books and Gifts), and also houses a conference center.

Description: St. Andrew's Abbey is in the northern foothills of the San Gabriel Mountains on the edge of the Mojave Desert, at an altitude of 3,600 feet. Here the summers are hot, winter days are sunny and the nights are cold, and spring blossoms with wildflowers. The abbey's buildings, contemporary in design, are set in a wooded area. St. Andrew's is known worldwide for its ceramics, and these are exhibited and sold at the monastery shop. Stations of the Cross are along the hillside on the abbey grounds.

Special Note: St. Andrew's Abbey sponsors workshops, group retreats, and days of recollection. Contact the abbey's guest master for more information. "You will be asked to make a non-refundable/non-transferable deposit to reserve your room. If you cancel, your deposit will be considered a charitable donation and deposited in our scholarship fund."

> *The word which came to Jeremiah from the Lord, saying Arise, and go down to the potter's house, and there I will cause thee to hear my words.*
>
> —JEREMIAH 18:1-2

St. Francis House

3743 Cesar Chavez St., San Francisco CA 94110

Order: Community of St. Francis (Episcopal)

Contact: Guest Sister

Telephone: 415-824-0288; fax: 415-826-7569

Web site: www.communitystfrancis.org; **e-mail:** csfsfo@aol.com

Accommodations: One twin-bedded apartment with private bath accommodates up to two guests.

Meals: Self-catering

Costs: $50 per day for room

Directions: From downtown San Francisco, take US 101 South to Cesar Chavez exit. Go west on Cesar Chavez St. just past Guerrero St.

From San Francisco International Airport, take I-280 to the San Jose exit. Go past first stoplight and turn left on Dolores St. Continue nine blocks to Cesar Chavez St. Turn right. St. Francis House is in middle of block.

Public Transportation: Take J Church streetcar to 27th St. stop. It is then a two-block walk to St. Francis House. Alternately, take BART (Bay Area Rapid Transit) subway to 24th and Mission. It is then a 10-minute walk to house.

History: The Community of St. Francis is a part of the Anglican Franciscan Society of St. Francis. The community was founded in 1905 in England, and its members live a life of prayer, study, and work among the poor and marginalized.

Description: St. Francis House is a fine example of a 1930s San Francisco art deco–style house. The guest apartment, on the first floor, overlooks a garden. St. Francis House is an urban community house, located in the historic Mission District near San Francisco's Hispanic neighborhood.

Points of Interest: A popular tourist destination, San Francisco has some exceptionally beautiful cathedrals: Grace Episcopal Cathedral on Nob Hill (Gothic Revival), the Roman Catholic Cathedral of St. Mary of the Assumption (strikingly modern), and the onion-domed Holy Virgin Russian Orthodox Cathedral. Mission Dolores (founded 1776), Chinatown, Golden Gate Bridge and Park, Fisherman's Wharf, and Alcatraz are also popular sites.

Santa Sabina Center

25 Magnolia Ave., San Rafael, CA 94901

Order: Dominican Sisters of San Rafael (Roman Catholic)

Contact: Guest Sister

Telephone: 415-457-7724. **Best time to call:** Mon. to Fri., 9 AM to 5 PM Pacific Time

Web site: www.sanrafaelop.org/whatwedo/santasabinaretreatcenter.htm; **e-mail:** info@santasabinacenter.org

Accommodations: Center can house up to 58 guests in 18 single and 20 twin-bedded rooms, two of which have private baths. There is also a straw-bale hermitage for one person, and a yurt set on a wooded hillside.

Meals: Meals are provided only for those participating in group retreats

Costs: Contact the center for current charges

Directions: Santa Sabina Center abuts Dominican University. From points north or south, take US 101 to the Central San Rafael exit. Follow sign to central San Rafael. Turn left on Mission Ave., and left again on Grand Ave. Make a slight right and then a slight left onto Palm Ave. Palm Ave. becomes Magnolia Ave.

Public Transportation: From San Francisco International Airport there are buses (Marin Airporter and Santa Rosa Airporter) to the San Rafael Transit Center. Alternately, there are Golden Gate Transit buses to the San Rafael Transit Center from San Francisco and Sonoma and Marin counties, and from the Richmond and El Cerrito BART (Bay Area Rapid Transit) stations in the East Bay. It is about a 1-mile walk or short cab ride from the Transit Center to Santa Sabina (there is a taxi stand on Tamalpais Ave. outside Transit Center). Another option on weekdays is the Golden Gate Transit Bus 49 (Novato–San Rafael Transit Center southbound). It stops at the corner of Grand and Arcaia Aves. in San Rafael, which is close to the university and Santa Sabina.

History: The Dominican Sisters opened Santa Sabina in 1939 as a house for their spiritual formation. This has been a retreat center since 1970.

Description: The center is a Tudor and Gothic Revival building. Its cloister encloses an interior garden, and there are more gardens to explore on the grounds. Next door is the 100-acre campus of Dominican University, where there are trails, wooded areas, and views of San Francisco Bay and its bridges.

Points of Interest: Santa Sabina is in Marin County near the Muir Woods National Monument and Mount Tamalpais. It is just 11 miles from San Francisco. The Napa Valley wine country is to the north.

Special Note: The center's heritage, focus, and motto is "a contemplative way of being."

Villa Maria del Mar

2-1918 E. Cliff Dr., Santa Cruz, CA 95062

Order: Sisters of the Holy Names of Jesus and Mary (Roman Catholic)

Contact: Guest Sister

Telephone: 831-475-1236. **Best time to call:** Mon. to Fri., 9 AM to 5 PM Pacific Time

Web site: www.villamariadelmar.org; **e-mail:** villamariadelmar@earth link.net

Accommodations: Two guest houses accommodate up to 70 individuals, in single, twin, and doubled-bedded rooms. Each room has private bath.

Meals: Three "home cooked healthy meals" daily

Costs: $97 per person per night for room and three meals, single occupancy; $87 per person per night for room and three meals, double occupancy. Weekend rate (Fri. evening to Sun. afternoon) is $218 per person, single, and $197 per person, double.

Directions: From points north, take CA 17 South to CA 1 South toward Monterey/Watsonville. Exit at Soquel Ave. Make an immediate left at signal onto 17th Ave. In 2 miles you will cross Portola Dr. and 17th Ave. becomes E. Cliff Dr. It is then two blocks to the Villa.

From points south, take CA 1 North toward Santa Cruz. Exit at 41st Ave. Turn left at signal. Continue 2 miles on 41st to Portola Ave. Turn right at Portola, then left on 19th Ave. Go one block and turn left on E. Cliff Ave. The Villa driveway will be on right.

Public Transportation: There is bus service (Santa Cruz Airport Flyer) from San Jose International Airport to Santa Cruz. Contact the guest sister for additional information.

History: The Sisters of the Holy Names of Jesus and Mary were founded in France in 1823 and came to work in California in 1868. They have owned this property for nearly a half century, and began welcoming guests here in 1963.

Description: The Villa Maria del Mar enjoys a site overlooking Monterey Bay. There are views of the bay from many vantage points including the Surfside Dining Room. The landscaped property has walking paths along the waterfront. The chapel is more than 100 years old.

Points of Interest: Santa Cruz was the site of one of the missions built in the 1700s by Father Junípero Serra. A half-size replica of the mission may be visited on the grounds of Holy Cross Church at the city's plaza. The area is also home to the Santa Cruz Museum of Art and History, Santa Cruz Historical Trust Museum, the Santa Cruz Surfing Museum, Santa Cruz Museum of Natural History, Seymour Marine Discovery Center, the city's beach boardwalk, and the Natural Bridges State Beach, with its multitude of monarch butterflies.

Special Note: The villa is closed to guests on Sunday nights.

✤ COLORADO

Abbey of St. Walburga

1029 Benedictine Way, Virginia Dale, CO 80536-7632

Order: Benedictine Nuns (Roman Catholic)

Contact: Sister Maria-Benedicta, O.S.B.

Telephone: 970-472-0612. Best times to call: 9 AM to 11 AM and 2:30 PM to 4:30 PM Mountain Time

Web site: www.walburga.org; **e-mail:** retreats@walburga.org

Accommodations: Main guest house accommodates 20 individuals, each in a single room. A smaller modular guest house has three single and two double rooms for up to seven guests.

Meals: Three meals daily

Costs: $55 per person per day for room and three meals. Group rates are slightly higher.

Directions: Virginia Dale is north of Denver, near the Colorado/Wyoming state border. From Denver, take I-25 North to Ft. Collins and then take Exit CO 14 (West). CO 14 and US 287 are the same road through Ft. Collins.

Follow the signs for US 287, which will bring you to Virginia Dale (about 40 miles north of Ft. Collins).

Public Transportation: There is no public transportation to Virginia Dale.

History: This community has its roots in the ancient Abbey of St. Walburg in Eichstatt, Bavaria. Founded in the 1930s, the monastery was in Boulder for nearly 70 years, moving to its present, more remote home in 1997. Today the abbey has 24 cloistered, contemplative nuns from the U.S., Germany, Canada, and the Philippines. The nuns support themselves through their guest house ministry, farming, raising cattle, selling natural grass-fed beef, gift shop, productions from St. Walburga Press, and altar bread distribution. The nuns also produce various artworks and other crafts: rosaries, coffins and burial urns, calligraphy, and weaving.

Description: Built in 1999, the abbey enjoys a quiet, secluded location in a valley where it is surrounded by rocky crags and beautiful canyons.

Points of Interest: The Abbey of St. Walburga is in northern Colorado, where the high plains meet the foothills of the Rocky Mountains. Within driving distance are the historic towns of Laramie and Cheyenne, Wyoming.

Special Note: "All guests are welcome to participate in the Divine Office, which we sing daily."

> *Levavi oculos meos in montes,*
> *Unde veniet auxilium mihi.*
>
> *I will lift up mine eyes unto the hills,*
> *From whence cometh my help.*
>
> —PSALM 12

St. Benedict's Monastery

1012 Monastery Rd., Snowmass, CO 81654

Order: Cistercian (Trappist) Monks (Roman Catholic)

Contact: Guest Master

Telephone: 970-927-1162

Web site: www.stbenedictsretreat.com; **e-mail:** retreat@rof.net

Accommodations: Gatehouse can accommodate three guests, each in a single room with shared bath. Retreat center accommodates up to 20 guests in 10 self-contained units (with kitchenette and bath).

Meals: Guests prepare their own meals

Costs: Suggested donation $40 per person per night

Directions: From Denver, take I-70 West to Glenwood Springs, then CO 82 from Glenwood Springs to Old Snowmass, which is 2.5 miles past Basalt. Turn right at intersection where there is a Conoco gas station/Snowmass Deli. Then drive straight for about 7.5 miles. Turn right at intersection of Snowmass Creek and Capital Creek Rds. In 7.5 miles turn left at sign for monastery onto Monastery Rd. and travel 1 mile to gatehouse, which is next to a large wooden arch spanning the road. Retreat house is up road on left. Monastery is straight ahead.

Public Transportation: There is air service to Aspen, and Amtrak trains and Greyhound buses go to Glenwood Springs. Arrange with the guest master in advance to be met at the airport, depot, or station.

Description: Set in a valley at an elevation of 8,000 feet, St. Benedict's Monastery property is extensive and includes a ranch, streams, hills, aspen forests, and meadowlands. The monastery abuts a national forest. The monks work on their ranch and in their greenhouse. The retreat center has a chapel/meditation hall, a library, conference rooms, a kitchen, and a dining room. A photo of the monastery at sunset is on the cover of this book.

> *Let the care of the guest house, also, be entrusted to a brother whose soul is possessed with the fear of God: let there be sufficient beds prepared there and let the house of God be wisely governed by prudent men.*
>
> —RULE OF SAINT BENEDICT

✤ CONNECTICUT

Convent of St. Birgitta
Vikingsborg
4 Runkenhage Rd., Darien, CT 06820

Order: Sisters of St. Birgitta (Roman Catholic)

Contact: Guest Sister

Telephone: 203-655-1068

Web site: www.birgittines-us.com; **e-mail:** convent@birgittines-us.com or conventsb@optonline.net

Accommodations: Vikingsborg houses up to 12 guests in single and twin rooms, each with private bath. In addition, six guests may be accommodated in three twin rooms in the cottage.

Meals: Three meals daily

Costs: Per person, room and three meals $110; room and breakfast only, $90. The cost for a day visit (no overnight stay) is $40 for lunch or dinner.

Directions: From New York, New Jersey, and southern Connecticut, take I-95 to Exit 12; turn right onto Tokeneke Rd. Proceed 0.5 mile on Tokeneke Rd. to intersection island; bear right around island to Old Farm Rd. and proceed 0.5 mile to Runkenhage Rd. (note green shield-shaped sign on left of road). Turn onto Runkenhage and go to first driveway on right (about 50 feet from turn); drive through two sets of stone posts in the direction of sign reading "Vikingsborg."

Public Transportation: From Manhattan's Grand Central Station take Metro North commuter rail to Darien, Connecticut. Taxis are available at station at each train arrival. The convent is about 1.75 miles from station.

History: The patron and namesake of this order is St. Birgitta of Sweden. She was born to a noble family in 1303 and became widely known through her written *Revelations*. The order she founded flourished in northern Europe during the Middle Ages and then became nearly extinct following the Reformation. The Birgittine Sisters began an era of resurgence and growth in the early 20th century and in 1957 four sisters arrived in Darien to take up residence at Vikingsborg.

Description: The beautifully appointed guest house is close to woodland walks and gardens, and guests enjoy "the peace, silence, serenity, and beauty that surrounds the whole place . . ."

Points of Interest: Vikingsborg is "nestled within hidden inlets of the Long Island Sound."

Special Note: The convent does not schedule retreats, but retreat groups of all denominations are welcome to come with their own director for days of recollection, meditation, study, discussion, or workshop. Literature and information are available from the convent's guest sister.

Monastery of the Glorious Cross

61 Burban Dr., Branford, CT 06405

Order: Benedictines of Jesus Crucified (Roman Catholic)

Contact: Guest House Director

Telephone: 203-315-9964 or 203315-0106. Best times to call: 10 AM to 11:30 AM, 1:30 PM to 5:30 PM, and 7:30 PM to 8:30 PM Eastern Time

Web site: www.benedictinesjc.org/gloriouscross.html; **e-mail:** monastery gc@juno.com

Accommodations: Guest wing of the monastery accommodates 10 persons in six single and two twin-bedded rooms, all with shared baths.

Meals: The main meal of the day is served at noon. Breakfast and supper foods are supplied and may be heated in the guest wing kitchenette microwave oven. "Some guests prefer to go out for their evening meal."

Costs: Suggested donation of $35 to $40 per person per day for room and meals.

Directions: From points south take I-95 North to Exit 51 (East Haven) to US 1. Continue past a few intersections (Lake Saltonstall will be on left) to Jefferson Rd. (McDonald's is at corner). Turn right onto Jefferson and drive to end, where it meets Burban Dr. Turn right onto Burban and then make an immediate left to monastery driveway. Continue around building to the two redbrick square pillars in front. This is the main entrance. Upon arrival, ring doorbell.

From points north, take I-95 South to Exit 54 (Cedar St.). Turn left off ramp. At second light make a right onto US 1 (Main St.). Continue for eight stoplights until you see a left-turn zone. Harley-Davidson and Honda dealerships will be on left. At light turn left onto Jefferson Rd. and then continue as above.

Public Transportation: There is bus and train service to Union Station in New Haven. It is then a 10–15-minute cab ride to monastery. There is air service to Tweed Airport in New Haven. From there it is a 10-minute cab ride to monastery. From Bradley International Airport in Hartford, take Connecticut Limo to New Haven and then a taxi to monastery.

History: The Benedictines of Jesus Crucified are a community of nuns founded in France in 1930 with an opening toward women with certain physical limitations, as well as those in good health. They moved to this location in 2001, combining communities that had lived in Devon, Pennsylvania, and Newport, Rhode Island. The building once housed The Connecticut Hospice, the first hospice in America.

Description: The monastery is a modern redbrick one-story building surrounded by eight acres with adjoining woodland. The sisters own the small Lion's Park, which is available to guests.

Points of Interest: The monastery is about 1 mile from Long Island Sound. Yale University, with its historic campus and many attractions, is located nearby in New Haven.

Special Note: "The sisters sing the Liturgy of the Hours daily, and have daily Mass on site. Guests are encouraged to attend Mass and the Offices. The Chapel is always open for their private prayer as well."

Come to me, all who labour and are heavy laden, and I will give you rest.

—MATTHEW 11:28

St. Edmund's Retreat
Ender's Island

P.O. Box 399, 99 Yacht Club Rd., Mystic, CT 06355

Order: Edmunite Fathers and Brothers (Roman Catholic)

Contact: Reservations Office

Telephone: 860-536-0565, ext. 167

Web site: www.endersisland.com; **e-mail:** programs@endersisland.com

Accommodations: Enders House and three other buildings accommodate up to 70 guests in single or double rooms, most with shared baths.

Meals: Three "quality and delicious meals" daily

Costs: $85 per person per night for room and meals. The rate drops to $80 per night if the stay is five nights or longer.

Directions: Enders Island is 4 miles from the center of Mystic. Take I-95 to Exit 90 (Mystic). Proceed south on US 27 to US 1. Turn left on US 1 (north); at first traffic light, turn left onto Mason's Island Rd. Bear left at all forks and follow signs to Enders Island.

Public Transportation: There is bus, Amtrak, and ferry service to Mystic. The nearest airports are Groton–New London, Connecticut, and T. F. Green Airport in Providence, Rhode Island. Contact the Retreat or visit Web site for further information.

History: The Edmundites were founded in 1843 and named for Saint Edmund Rich, a 13th-century Archbishop of Canterbury. The island once belonged to Dr. and Mrs. Thomas B. Enders. Here they built their mansion home about a century ago. In 1954 Mrs. Enders gave Enders Island to the Edmundites.

Description: St. Edmund's Retreat is sited on an 11-acre private island connected to the mainland by a bridge. It is "one of the few places in New England where you can awake to the sounds of seabirds calling, waves lapping, and a mass bell pealing." Surrounded by gardens and pathways, the Main House is the former Enders mansion, in which some of the guests lodge. It is an arts and crafts–style building, and includes guest rooms as well as a little Fisherman's Chapel. A recently built addition to the island is the Chapel of Our Lady of the Assumption, which has been called "a pilgrimage in its own right." The chapel contains works by the artists of St. Michael Institute of Sacred Art. The institute, another ministry of St. Edmund's, exists "to preserve and promote the highest standards of excellence in the sacred arts" and has programs in Gregorian chant, iconography, manuscript illumination, marble mosaics, stained glass, traditional drawing, and calligraphy.

Points of Interest: Nearby is Mystic Seaport, a re-creation of an 1800s New England waterfront village. The *Charles W. Morgan,* the sole surviving 19th-century American whaling ship, is docked there. Mystic Aquarium & Institute for Exploration is also here. The town was the setting for the 1988 film *Mystic Pizza,* starring Julia Roberts.

Special Note: In the words of the Edmundites, Enders Island is "easy to get to; hard to leave."

✤ DISTRICT OF COLUMBIA

Georgetown Visitation Monastery

1500 35th St., NW, Washington, DC 20007

Order: Visitation Sisters (Roman Catholic)

Contact: Guest Sister

Telephone: 202-337-0305

Web site: www.georgetownvisitation.org; **e-mail:** GVMonastery@gmail.com

Accommodations: Monastery houses two female guests, each in a single room with shared bath.

Meals: Three meals daily

Costs: "Donations gladly accepted"

Directions: The monastery is in northwest Washington, at the corner of 35th St. and P St.

Public Transportation: The nearest Metrorail stops are Rosslyn (Blue and Orange lines) and DuPont Circle (Red Line). Metrobuses G2, D2, and D6 go to the monastery.

History: Saint Francis de Sales, bishop of Geneva, and Saint Jane de Chantal, a widowed baroness, founded the Order of the Visitation of Holy Mary in 1610. Georgetown Visitation Monastery began in 1799 and is the second-oldest monastery for women in America. Its mission was the education of young women, a work that the nuns continue today at Georgetown Visitation Preparatory School.

Description: The monastery is a handsome Federal redbrick building buffered from the city with adjacent green space.

Points of Interest: Georgetown University is just steps from the monastery. Other sites in Georgetown include Dumbarton Oaks Museum and Gardens, Dumbarton House, Tudor Place, the Old Stone House, the Chesapeake and Ohio Canal, and Holy Trinity Catholic Church (built in

1851), which John and Jackie Kennedy attended while Georgetown residents. Washington National Cathedral is nearby, and the Basilica of the National Shrine of the Immaculate Conception is 6 miles east of the monastery.

Special Note: The guest rooms at the monastery are for retreats only. The sisters have daily Mass and sing the Liturgy of the Hours five times a day.

St. Anselm's Abbey

4501 South Dakota Ave., NE, Washington, DC 20017

Order: Benedictine Monks (Roman Catholic)

Contact: Guest Master

Telephone: 202-269-2300

Web site: www.stanselms.org; **e-mail:** abbeyandguests@stanselms.org

Accommodations: Monastery houses eight male guests in single rooms with shared bath. One suite with a private bath is available to one or two women. Guests "with a spiritual purpose are welcome for brief visits."

Meals: Three meals daily

Costs: An offering of at least $30 per person per day for room and meals is suggested.

Directions: Contact guest master for driving directions.

Public Transportation: Take Metrorail Red Line to Brookland-CUA. From there take the R4 bus to 14th St. Cross South Dakota Ave. and walk one block to abbey gates. Alternately, you may take the 80 bus in the direction of Ft. Totten and get off at Allison St., then walk two blocks to South Dakota Ave.

History: St. Anselm's was founded in 1923 by monks from the Abbey of Fort Augustus in Scotland. They bought a farm on this site because of its proximity to the Catholic University of America. By 1930 a new monastery was built in the English Tudor style. A second, more modern wing was added in 1964. St. Anselm's has had a day school for boys since 1942.

Description: The redbrick abbey church with its wooden choir stalls and stained-glass windows is reminiscent of English prototypes. The abbey's landscaped grounds are a peaceful refuge in urban Washington.

Points of Interest: The abbey is close to the massive Basilica of the National Shrine of the Immaculate Conception. Also nearby is the Franciscan Monastery, which has replicas of Roman catacombs and Holy Land sites and shrines. The Washington Metro provides fast and easy access to the Washington National Cathedral and other points of religious, cultural, patriotic, historic, and educational interest.

❖ FLORIDA

Holy Name Monastery

P.O. Box 2450, 33201 Highway 52 East,
St. Leo, FL 33574-2450

Order: Benedictine Sisters of Florida (Roman Catholic)

Contact: Program Coordinator

Telephone: 352-588-8320

Web site: www.floridabenedictines.com; **e-mail:** holyname@stleo.edu

Accommodations: Monastery houses up to 16 guests in single rooms, all with shared baths.

Meals: Guests are asked to make arrangements with the monastery for meal service.

Costs: $60 per person per day for single room and meals; $50 per person per day for double room with meals; $20 per person per day for room only.

Directions: From I-75, take Exit 59 and go east on FL 52 for approximately 3 miles.

From I-4, take Exit 18 and go north on US 98 to FL 52 (30 miles).

Public Transportation: The nearest airport is Tampa International Airport. Contact program coordinator for further information.

History: In 1889 the settlers of Florida's Catholic Colony of San Antonio invited Benedictine sisters from Pennsylvania. Five accepted the invitation and opened Holy Name Academy. The monastery now numbers 18 sisters.

Description: Located on 100 acres of gently rolling hills, the monastery is a modern building overlooking scenic Lake Jovita. This quiet and peaceful area, with palm trees and orange groves, extends into the adjoining property of St. Leo Abbey and St. Leo University. Recreational facilities on campus include a swimming pool, tennis courts, and a golf course.

Points of Interest: Walt Disney World, Busch Gardens, the John F. Kennedy Space Center, Cypress Gardens, and other sites are an hour or so from the monastery.

Special Note: In addition to welcoming individual guests, the monastery also offers group retreats. Contact the program coordinator for more information.

Riverside Retreat

7305 County Rd. 78, LaBelle, FL 33935

Order: United Methodist Church

Contact: Martha Pierce, Director

Telephone: 863-675-0334. **Best time to call:** 8 AM to 3:30 PM Eastern Time, Mon. to Fri.

Web site: www.riversideretreatumchurchcamp.com; **e-mail:** mpierce riverside@yahoo.com

Accommodations: Up to 150 guests can be accommodated. There are several options including a guest house, lodges, tent camping, and RV camping. All have shared baths.

Meals: Food service may be arranged in advance for large groups only.

Costs: Fees vary from $16 to $28 per person per night for room only.

Directions: LaBelle is west of Palm Beach and east of Fort Myers near FL 80. Contact director for detailed directions.

Public Transportation: Fort Myers International Airport is 35 miles away. Contact the director for further information.

History: Riverside Retreat was founded as a Methodist church camp in the mid-1950s.

Description: The retreat occupies 150 acres stretching along a half mile of the Caloosahatchee River shoreline. Its open meadows and corridors of grass are surrounded by forests of live oak, palm, cypress, pine, and other trees. It is a place for relaxation, meditation, exercise, and fun.

Special Note: There are many outdoor recreation options, including fishing, kayaking, biking, hiking, swimming, picnicking, archery, volleyball, basketball, hayrides, low ropes, and nature exploration.

It's the nature of the place.

—RIVERSIDE RETREAT MOTTO

St. Leo Abbey

P.O. Box 2350, 33601 State Rd. 52, St. Leo, FL 33574

Order: Benedictine Monks (Roman Catholic)

Contact: Guest Master

Telephone: 352-588-8184

Web site: www.saintleoabbey.org; **e-mail:** abbey@saintleo.edu

Accommodations: Guest House accommodates eight, in two single and three double rooms.

Meals: Three meals daily. Guests dine with the monks.

Costs: $60 per room per night, single occupancy, meals included, or $75 per room per night, double occupancy, meals included.

Directions: From Tampa, take I-75 North to Exit 285 (San Antonio, St. Leo). Turn right onto FL 52 and continue east to the township of St. Leo. Turn left at entrance to Holy Name Monastery, then make an immediate right and follow service road to St. Leo Abbey.

Public Transportation: There is bus service to Dade City. From Tampa International Airport it is a 45-minute drive to abbey. There is limousine service from airport to abbey (or arrange with the guest master in advance for pickup).

History: St. Leo Abbey dates to 1889, when monks from Belmont Abbey, North Carolina, arrived in central Florida. They established a military school, then a preparatory school, and in 1959, St. Leo University. Today the community numbers 22 monks.

Description: The abbey church is popularly known as the church that was built with orange juice, as the cost of construction was largely defrayed by income from the abbey's citrus groves. It is Lombard Romanesque in design, its wooden appointments derived from the abbey's cedar trees. A 2,100-pound marble crucifix is the focal point of the sanctuary. Guests may stroll the walkways through 50 acres of woods along the shores of Lake Jovita. Beyond is some of the most beautiful countryside in Florida.

Points of Interest: Florida's beaches are but an hour from the abbey, and Walt Disney World, Universal Studios, and the Salvador Dali Museum are each an hour and a half away. Busch Gardens is 40 minutes away. The John F. Kennedy Space Center is two and a half hours from here.

Special Note: In addition to the guest house, St. Leo's Abbey also offers the Retreat House to groups. Contact the guest master for more information.

❖ GEORGIA

Convent of St. Helena

3042 Eagle Dr., Augusta, GA 30906-3326

Order: Order of St. Helena (Episcopal)

Contact: Guest Coordinator

Telephone: 706-798-5201

Web site: www.osh.org; **e-mail:** sisters@osh.org

Accommodations, Meals, and Costs: For information contact the guest coordinator.

Directions: Take I-20 to Exit 196A to I-520 (Bobby Jones Expressway). Take I-520 to Exit 5B (US 1 North, Deans Bridge Rd). Turn right at second traffic light (at the 76 Circle K station) onto Lumpkin Rd. Continue on Lumpkin Rd. past one traffic light and two Shelby Rd. turns. Turn right onto Green Meadows Dr. (note Cheeks Tax Service). Green Meadows Dr. ends at a T at Eagle Dr.; turn left. Continue on Eagle Dr. up steep hill past dead end sign. At Episcopal Church sign veer to right onto convent property. Parking lot is around bend.

Public Transportation: Delta and US Airways have service to Augusta Regional Airport. Southeastern Stages has bus service to Augusta. Contact guest coordinator in advance if you wish to be met on arrival.

History: The Order of St. Helena was founded in Kentucky in 1945 and has had convents in New York City; Vails Gate, New York; and Seattle. The convent in Augusta was built in 1962. The 20 sisters in Augusta witness to a contemporary version of traditional monasticism and their lives are dedicated to prayer and service. The sisters sing the Divine Office in the traditional style of Gregorian chant.

Description: The modern chapel has clear glass walls that look out onto the convent's landscaped property, displaying a wide variety of flora and fauna. The 20-acre site has walking trails, a labyrinth, and a gazebo.

Points of Interest: Augusta is home to the annual Masters Golf Tournament. Downtown Augusta has St. Paul's Episcopal Church, which dates to 1750, as well as several museums. The banks of the Savannah River, both in Georgia and across the way in South Carolina, are lined with pleasant river walks. Another way to enjoy the serenity of the river is on a barge or boat ride.

Special Note: The convent offers many day guest programs such as Saturday retreats, workshops, quiet days, spiritual direction, psychotherapy, and healing touch. "We offer our facility to other organizations for day group retreats."

Monastery of Our Lady of the Holy Spirit
2625 Highway 212 SW, Conyers, GA 30094-4044

Order: Cistercian (Trappist) Monks (Roman Catholic)

Contact: Registrar

Telephone: 770-760-0959. Best times to call: Mon. to Fri. 8 AM to 4 PM Eastern Time

Web site: www.trappist.net; **e-mail:** rhouse@trappist.net

Accommodations: Retreat house accommodates up to 40 guests in single rooms, all with shared baths.

Meals: Three meals daily

Costs: $60–$100 per person per day for room and meals. There is a $30 registration fee, which is applied toward first night's stay.

Directions: From downtown Atlanta, take I-20 East to Exit 37. Turn right onto Panola Rd. and go 2.3 miles to fourth traffic light. Turn left onto Brown's Mill Rd. (GA 212). Continue 9.5 miles to monastery, which will be on left.

Public Transportation: Access Atlanta shuttle service (call 770-713-4789) will pick up at Atlanta airport, train, or bus station with advance notice.

History: The monks acquired Honey Creek Plantation in 1944. At first they lived in a barn loft, but with hard work, prayer, and imagination, the monks transformed the former plantation into an abbey, complete with church, bell tower, and cloistered quadrangle.

Description: About 30 miles from downtown Atlanta, the abbey is a place of austere beauty and solitude. The abbey church, of modified Gothic design, has a quiet, serene interior lit by rows of stained-glass windows. It took a quarter century to build and complete the abbey.

Point of Interest: Stone Mountain is nearby.

✦ IDAHO

Marymount Hermitage

2150 Hermitage Ln., Mesa, ID 83643-5005

Order: Hermit Sisters of Mary (Roman Catholic)

Contact: Sister Mary Beverly, H.S.M.

Telephone: 208-256-4354 (messages only)

Web site: www.marymount-hermitage.org; **e-mail:** marymount@ctc web.net

Accommodations: Five guests are housed in single hermitages with private baths.

Meals: Three meals daily (self-prepared in the hermitages)

Costs: $40 for room and meals

Directions: Marymount Hermitage is located west of US 95 between Council and Cambridge, midway between mile markers 128 and 129, just north of the town of Mesa. ("Be sure to arrive before sunset as there are no streetlights in the area.")

Public Transportation: There is air service to Boise (two and a half hours away) and bus service to New Meadows, Idaho (one hour north). A neighbor of the hermitage, with prior notice and for cash payment, provides car service from these towns for the following round-trip fees: Boise, $200; Ontario, Oregon, $150; and New Meadows $100.

History: The eremitical (i.e., hermit) tradition in Christian monasticism is centuries old, inspired by the lives and teachings of the Desert Fathers. With a reverence for this tradition and in an authentic spirit of renewal, Marymount Hermitage was solemnly dedicated in 1984. At first Marymount included three hermitages, a chapel, library, and a common house. In 1987 the bell tower rang its first peal, and two additional hermitages were built the following year. "Our Father's House," the new chapel, was dedicated in 1994.

Description: On 100 acres of rolling, high-desert rangeland, Marymount is at an elevation of 3,200 feet. Surrounded by mountains, the hermitage itself is on a mesa overlooking a valley 200 feet below. Look for wildlife such as birds, rabbits, and deer. There are also coyotes, small rodents, lizards, and snakes, which the sisters assure us are harmless!

Special Note: "We send out a free newsletter to explain the spirituality and material progress of Marymount Hermitage."

✤ ILLINOIS

Benedictine Priory of Christ the King
P.O. Box 409090, Chicago, IL 60640

Order: Benedictines of Christ the King (Anglican)

Contact: Brother Kirt, O.S.B.

Telephone: 773-907-8200. **Best time to call:** 9 AM to noon, Central Time

Accommodations: Priory or parish facilities house two male guests in single rooms with shared bath.

Meals: Self-prepared in the kitchen or sometimes shared at a local neighborhood restaurant

Costs: $25 per person per night

Directions: The priory is on the north-central side of Chicago. Contact the priory for directions.

Public Transportation: Available, but not advised for persons new to area because of high crime rate.

History: The first brothers took vows in 1970. The Benedictines of Christ the King were established in Chicago's inner city in 1985, and maintain a strong affiliation with the nearby St. Paul's-by-the-Lake Episcopal Church. "Our apostolate is the promotion of biblical discipleship in coordination with the Rule of St. Benedict. We are keenly interested in both sound scholarship and practical 'hands on' ministry to the poor and disadvantaged." The brothers also have a ministry in Sydney, Australia.

Description: The priory has a chapel for prayerful meditation, and it maintains a small library.

Special Note: Only directed retreats are scheduled at the priory, and these are usually coordinated with liturgical services. Contact the priory for details. "Both brothers and guests are required to work in some form of purposeful labor while visiting, as well as time spent in study and prayer. The brothers also request that sightseeing in Chicago be reserved for either before or after the retreat itself."

Monastery of the Holy Cross

3111 S. Aberdeen St., Chicago, IL 60608-6503

Order: Benedictine Monks (Roman Catholic)

Contact: Guest Master

Telephone: 773-927-7424, ext. 202, or 888-539-4261, ext. 202.

Web site: www.chicagomonk.org; **e-mail:** porter@chicagomonk.org

Accommodations: The monastery's guest facilities include the Benedictine Bed and Breakfast, which has two private apartments: St. Joseph Loft and Bethany Garden House, each with private entrance. Both are air-conditioned. St. Joseph Loft has three bedrooms (two doubles and one single), as well as a living room, kitchenette, breakfast room, and bath. Bethany Garden House has two bedrooms (one double and one single), a living room (with futon that serves as a double bed), dining room, full kitchen, and bath, as well as a spacious outdoor deck that opens onto the monastery's garden. Another accommodation is the Monastery Guest House, which accommodates up to six guests and "provides a place of silence and prayer in the midst of the city for those who seek God in retreat. Guests are able to join the monks for the chanting of the Divine Office throughout the day and for the celebration of the Mass."

Meals: Guests staying in St. Joseph Loft are served a full, hot breakfast prepared by the monks. In Bethany Garden House meals are self-catered; the refrigerator is stocked with breakfast foods. Guests staying at the Monastery Guest House are served three meals a day.

Costs: Bed and breakfast rates are $165 per night for 1–2 adults, $210 per night for 3–4 adults, and $255 per night for 5–6 adults. Children 18 and younger stay free of charge. In the Guest House the suggested offering is $40 per person per night for room and meals. There are extended-stay rates for five or more nights, corporate rates, an AARP discount, and an active-military discount. Corporate rates are available. MasterCard, Visa, and American Express are accepted.

Directions: From Dan Ryan Expressway (I-90/I-94), take Exit 54 (31st St. exit) and go west. Monastery is located at the corner of 31st and Aberdeen

Sts. (second church steeple west of expressway). Alternately, from Lake Shore Dr. (US 41) take 31st St. exit. (Third church steeple west of Lake Shore Dr. is the monastery's). Off-street parking in secure lot is provided.

Public Transportation: Midway Airport is 15 minutes away; O'Hare Airport is an hour away. From either airport take the CTA (Chicago Transit Authority) train to the Halsted Station on the Orange (Midway) Line. Pickup from this stop, which is 1 mile from monastery, can be arranged with advance notice. Or transfer to 62 Archer Bus heading west (bus stop is at curb directly in front of CTA station) and get off at Loomis St. Walk south two blocks on Loomis to monastery church.

History: In 1991 the late Joseph Cardinal Bernardin invited this Benedictine community to Chicago to take up residence at the former Immaculate Conception Church (which had been closed a year earlier). The monks have transformed the former parish church building, rectory, convent, and other facilities into a vibrant urban monastic center. Holy Cross has a close affiliation with the Monastery of Christ in the Desert, New Mexico.

Description: The monastery church is a massive century-old Gothic Revival structure. The spacious interior, lit by some of the finest stained-glass windows in Chicago, is embellished with a delicately carved wood reredos and hand-painted icons. Outside the church there is a walled cloister garden that guests find particularly inviting.

Points of Interest: The monastery is located in the Bridgeport neighborhood, just south of the Loop. This is an ethnically and racially diverse area with a wide variety of shops and restaurants. Close by is the McCormick Place Convention Complex, and White Sox Park is just 10 minutes away. Chinatown is also nearby. Just down the street (at the east end of 31st St.) is Lake Michigan, with its swimming beaches and extensive walking and biking paths. Farther afield, it is a 15-minute bus ride to downtown Chicago, with its many points of religious, cultural, and educational interest near the Chicago River.

> *There is a river, the steams whereof shall make glad the city of God . . .*

—PSALM 46

St. Benedict Abbey

7561 W. Lancaster Rd., Bartonville, IL 61607

Order: Benedictine Monks (ecumenical)

Contact: Guest Master

Telephone: 309-633-0057; fax: 309-633-0058. Best times to call: 9 AM to 11:40 AM and 1 PM to 4:40 PM Central Time

Web site: www.sbabbey.com; **e-mail:** sba@sbabbey.com

Accommodations: Abbey houses up to 12 guests in double-bedded rooms, all with shared baths.

Meals: Three meals daily

Costs: $45 per person per day for room and meals

Directions: From Peoria, take I-74 West in direction of Galesburg. Take Exit 87A (I-474 Indianapolis). Continue on I-474 for about 4 miles and take Exit 5 (Airport Rd.). At stoplight make left. Proceed on Airport Rd. (airport will be on right) for about 2 miles. Make right on Pfeiffer Rd.; Limestone Highway will be on corner. Exit Pfeiffer at Lancaster Rd. on left; monastery is on right in approximately 1.5 miles.

Public Transportation: There is air service to Peoria. Alternately, from Chicago's O'Hare Airport, the Peoria Charter Coach Company has shuttle service to Bradley University in Peoria. Pickup from Peoria can be arranged with prior notice.

History: St. Benedict Abbey has its roots in Puerto Rico. The community was founded there in 1985 by Dom J. Alberto Morales, and in 1996 it moved to Illinois where, as the monks have said, "God always sends angels to meet us."

Description: The abbey is in a quiet, pastoral setting surrounded by rolling fields.

Points of Interest: Peoria is home to the Forest Park Nature Center, the Wildlife Prairie Park, and the George L. Luthy Memorial Botanical Garden. Museums include the Lakeview Museum of Arts and Sciences, and the Wheels O' Time Museum. Illinois, the "Land of Lincoln," has sites related to the president's life in Springfield, the state capital, 70 miles north of the abbey.

❖ INDIANA

Divine Compassion House

311 Sixth St., Winona Lake, IN 46590

Order: Franciscan Missionaries of Divine Compassion (Anglican)

Contact: Sister Sarah, M.D.C.

Telephone: 574-269-5556

Web site: http://orders.anglican.org/mdc; **e-mail:** sistersarahmasters @yahoo.com

Accommodations: Convent and a guest apartment house nine guests in five rooms, all with shared baths.

Meals: Three meals daily

Costs: Suggested donation of $40 per person per day

Directions: From US 30 East, turn on Center St., driving toward Warsaw. Immediately get into left lane. Turn left on Argonne Rd. Drive under railroad overpass. Turn left onto King's Highway. Then turn right onto Sixth St.

Public Transportation: Contact Sister Sarah for information.

History: The Missionaries of Divine Compassion were founded in 2007 to "live authentic religious life while proclaiming the Catholic faith, as received by the Anglican Communion . . . bringing 'the Gospel to the people, the people to the sacraments, and the tender love of Jesus Christ to everyone.'" The sisters and friars have secular jobs and also perform a wide variety of ministries.

Description: The sisters and friars have transformed a 1950s brick ranch home into Divine Compassion House. It is one block from Grace College and Seminary, and three blocks from the Village at Winona. The house is within walking distance of a greenway and a public beach.

St. Meinrad Archabbey
Guest House

200 Hill Dr., St. Meinrad, IN 47577

Order: Benedictine Monks (Roman Catholic)

Contact: Brother Maurus Zoeller, O.S.B., Guest Master

Telephone: 812-357-66674 or 800-581-6905

Web site: www.saintmeinrad.edu; **e-mail:** mzoeller@saintmeinrad.edu

Accommodations: Archabbey Guest House accommodates up to 62 guests in 31 twin-bedded rooms, each with private bath.

Meals: Three meals daily

Costs: Rooms are $55 per day, single occupancy, and $75 per day, double occupancy. Meals are approximately $21 per day per person.

Directions: From points east, take I-64 West to Exit 72. Proceed south one block to IN 62. Turn right and drive 8 miles to St. Meinrad.

From the west take I-64 East to Exit 63. Drive south on IN 162 for 2.5 miles to flashing red light. Turn left on IN 62 and drive 4 miles to St. Meinrad.

Public Transportation: There is air service to Louisville and to Evansville. Contact guest master for further information.

History: St. Meinrad Archabbey was founded in 1854 by monks from Einsiedeln Abbey, Switzerland. Originally the monks ministered to the German-speaking Catholic immigrants and later expanded their ministry to the spiritual welfare and education of Native Americans. Today the abbey numbers more than 100 monks.

Description: The archabbey includes a college, a seminary, the Abbey Press publishing house, the Abbey Press Gift Shop, and the Scholar Shop bookstore. The monks also produce handcrafted wooden caskets and cremation urns. At the guest house you may obtain brochures and audio players for self-guided walking tours. There are also group guided tours, which start at the guest house every Saturday at 1:30 p.m. A mile away is the Monte Cassino Shrine, which was dedicated to the Virgin Mary by the monks in 1870.

> *Should there be artificers in the monastery, let them work*
> *at their crafts in all humility, if the abbot give permission.*
> —RULE OF SAINT BENEDICT

❖ IOWA

Abbey of St. Benedict

2288 220th St., Donnellson, IA 52625

Order: Companions of St. Luke—Benedictines (Episcopal)

Contact: Guest Master

Telephone: 319-837-8421

Web site: www.holythoughts.org; **e-mail:** abbotmichaeljohnaustin@ yahoo.com

Accommodations: Abbey houses 15 guests in single rooms, each with a private bath and climate control. There are additional accommodations in St. Anne House, with two bedrooms, private bath, living room, and kitchen.

Meals: Three meals daily

Costs: Suggested donation of $50 per person per day for room and meals, single occupancy; $75, double occupancy; and $75 for the suite with full-sized bed. In St. Anne House, it is $125 per person per night for room and meals, single occupancy.

Directions: From points north take US 218 South. From the east take US 34 West to US 218, and from the west take I-80 to US 218 South. Exit Route 218 South at sign for Donnellson and Ft. Madison. Turn left onto IA 2 and go about 6 miles. Turn left onto Golden Rd. and left again onto 220th St. Drive about 1 mile; look for big green sign for abbey on left. Follow sign to Hospitality Center and temporary parking.

Public Transportation: Contact guest master for information.

History: The community was located in Chicago for some years, and then relocated to its present home, completing phase one of its building program in 2008. There are 45 Companions, men and women, in the order today.

Description: "The Abbey is located in the splendor of God's beauty. Our Monastery sits within 35 acres of colorful gardens, thick woods, gentle streams, clear air, and a symphony of God's creatures."

Point of Interest: Old Fort Madison historic site is 7 miles from the abbey on the banks of the Mississippi River. Built in 1808, the fort has been restored and its costumed interpreters provide the visitor with a living-history frontier experience.

Mississippi Abbey

8400 Abbey Hill, Dubuque, IA 52003

Order: Cistercian (Trappistine) Nuns (Roman Catholic)

Contact: Guest Sister

Telephone: 563-582-2529. Call between 9 AM and 11:30 AM Central Time

Web site: www.ocso.org; **e-mail:** hospitality@olmabbey.org

Accommodations: Houses up to 11 women guests in single and twin rooms in three houses, all with shared baths

Meals: The nuns provide food for all the retreat houses, and guests cook their own meals.

Costs: Freewill offering accepted

Directions: The abbey is a 20-minute drive from Dubuque. From Dubuque take Locust St. (US 151/61 south) to US 52. Turn left (south) onto US 52 and go about 5 miles. Abbey sign will be on right, directing a left turn onto Hilken Hill Rd.

Public Transportation: There is air and bus service to Dubuque. Contact guest sister for more information.

History: The history of the Cistercian nuns closely parallels that of the monks of the same order. The Cistercians are an 11th-century reform of the Benedictines. A more austere reform was initiated at the abbey of La Trappe, France, in 1664. Nuns from Ireland opened the first Trappistine monastery in Wrentham, Massachusetts, in the mid-20th century. Thirteen nuns from Wrentham opened Mississippi Abbey in 1964.

Description: Mississippi Abbey is set on 580 acres, which includes bluffs, woods, and a creek, all of which guests are free to explore. The nuns run an organic farm on which they produce some of their own food. The nuns support themselves through the manufacture and sale of Trappistine Creamy Caramels.

Points of Interest: Jacques Marquette, a French priest, explored this area in the 17th century, and Dubuque was the first Roman Catholic archdiocese west of the Mississippi. One of the guest houses, the Stone House, is a farmhouse dating to the mid-1800s.

Special Note: The Stone House is open from March through October. The Retreat House is open January through November. The Cabin is open January through October. Retreats are usually booked two months in advance, although there are sometimes last-minute cancellations. Reservations are limited during the months of November and December because of the busy schedule at the candy house at that time.

New Melleray Abbey

6632 Melleray Circle, Peosta, IA 52068

Order: Cistercian (Trappist) Monks (Roman Catholic)

Contact: Guest Master

Telephone: 563-588-2319. Best times to call: 9:30 AM to 11:30 AM, 2 PM to 5 PM, or 6:15 PM to 7:15 PM Central Time

Web site: www.newmelleray.org; **e-mail:** guesthouse@newmelleray.org

Accommodations: Houses up to 26 guests in 18 single rooms and four double rooms, each with private bath.

Meals: Three meals daily

Costs: Suggested donation of $50 per person per day for room and meals

Directions: From Dubuque drive south on US 151 for about 17 miles. Turn right onto Monastery Rd./CR-D41. Make a right on Monastery Circle. Bear left at fork and continue on Monastery Circle. Abbey will be on left.

Public Transportation: There is air and Greyhound bus service to Dubuque. Contact guest master for further information.

History: The namesake of New Melleray Abbey is Mount Melleray Abbey in Ireland, from which the founding monks came in 1849.

Description: Enclosing a quadrangle, the monastery was built following a traditional monastic floor plan. Of particular note is the abbey church. Built in 1868 as a multistory wing of the monastery, it was gutted in 1976. The upper floors were removed, and the plaster stripped from the walls. The results are surprising and successful: a lofty abbey church of simple beauty and solid materials—stone walls and wooden rafters. Both church and monastery are surrounded by pine forests. Beyond are the cultivated fields where the monks farm.

Special Note: Guests are invited to New Melleray Abbey as a place of spiritual retreat.

✤ KANSAS

St. Benedict's Abbey
1020 N. 2nd St., Atchison, KS 66002

Order: Benedictine Monks (Roman Catholic)

Contact: Father Blaine Scultz, O.S.B., Guest Master

Telephone: 913-367-7853; Fax: 913-367-6230

Web site: www.kansasmonks.org; **e-mail:** blaine@benedictine.edu

Accommodations: Guest house accommodates up to 12 individuals in twin-bedded rooms, each with private bath.

Meals: Three meals daily

Costs: $40 per person per day for room and meals

Directions: From Kansas City, Missouri, or Kansas City International Airport, take I-29 North. At Platte City, take Exit 20 (Weston, Atchison, Leavenworth, and MO 273). Follow MO 273 until it joins MO 45 at red blinking light. Turn right, passing through outskirts of Weston. In about 15 miles you will see a small lake on left. Prepare to turn off 45 onto US 59 heading west. After 4 miles you will cross a bridge over the Missouri River and arrive in Atchison. At the foot of the bridge, turn right and cross the railroad tracks. At first red light, turn right for two blocks, then left onto Second St. In eight blocks you will see the twin-towered church of St. Benedict's parish. Proceed one more block north, then turn right at sign reading "Benedictine College." The new Student Activity Center is straight ahead of you. Follow winding road up hill to abbey, abbey church, and guest house complex on left. A curving parking lot is in front of guest house. Enter at double glass doors, where you will find information desk.

Public Transportation: No public transportation to abbey.

History: Monks arrived in Atchison in 1857, just two years after the former Indian Territory of Kansas was opened to settlers, and four years before Kansas was admitted to the Union as a state. Education has always been a primary mission of the monks here. St. Benedict's College (for men)

and Mount St. Scholastica College (for women) were combined in 1971 to form the coeducational Benedictine College. Today the college enrolls 1,350 students. The 55 monks of St. Benedict's Abbey teach, administer parishes, and are engaged in missionary work in Brazil.

Description: The abbey and guest house stand on a bluff high above the Missouri River. Here you'll find buildings with a wide variety of architectural styles. For example, the monastery, built in 1929, is a handsome Tudor Revival design. In 1957, a century after the monks' arrival, the present abbey church was built. A modern building, it is the work of architect Barry Byrne, a colleague of Frank Lloyd Wright. Inside the limestone edifice visitors will be impressed with the 270-foot-long nave, the 610-square-foot fresco by Jean Charlot, the outstanding organ (with 2,200 pipes), and the crypt below, with its chapels, shrines, and 28 altars dedicated to favorite saints.

Points of Interest: Atchison has many late-19th-century Victorian-style houses, churches, and public buildings. Just eight blocks from the abbey is the Amelia Earhart Birthplace Museum. Drop by the Santa Fe Depot Visitor Information Center (200 S. 10th) for maps of the city's historic walking and driving tours.

❖ KENTUCKY

Abbey of Gethsemani

3642 Monks Rd., Trappist, KY 40051

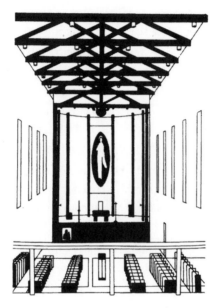

Order: Cistercian (Trappist) Monks (Roman Catholic)

Contact: Guest Master

Telephone: 502-549-4133

Web site: www.monks.org

Accommodations: Guest house accommodates up to 31 individuals in single or twin-bedded rooms, each with private bath. First and third weeks of the month are reserved for women; second and fourth weeks of the month are reserved for men.

Meals: Three meals daily

Costs: Freewill donations accepted

Directions: Take US 31E South from Bardstown, Kentucky, then turn left on KY 247.

Public Transportation: No public transportation to abbey.

History: In the 11th century the Cistercians began as a reform within the Benedictine order. In the 17th century a more austere reform was led by the French Abbot de Rance of La Grande Trappe Abbey. The Cistercians of the Strict Observance have since been popularly known as Trappists. A group of Trappist monks journeyed from France and settled in Kentucky in 1848.

Description: The abbey has an extensive property on which the monks farm and do other works such as the production and sale of cheeses and fruitcakes. Guests are welcome to walk in the gardens or woodlands and to join the monks for worship in the large and historic abbey church.

Point of Interest: Gethsemani Abbey was the home of Thomas Merton (1915–1968), the author of nearly 75 books and of poems, essays, and reviews. His best-known book is his autobiography, *The Seven Storey Mountain.*

Special Note: The weekend retreat is from Friday afternoon to Sunday afternoon or Monday morning. The midweek retreat is from Monday to Friday morning. Brochures are available on request.

Monks should love silence at all times . . .

—RULE OF SAINT BENEDICT

✤ LOUISIANA

St. Joseph Abbey

75376 River Rd., Covington, LA 70435

Contact: Brother Jude Israel, O.S.B., Guest Master

Order: Benedictine Monks (Roman Catholic)

Telephone: 985-892-1800. **Best time to call:** 9 AM to 5 PM Central Time

Web site: www.saintjosephabbey.com; **e-mail:** brJude@ajasc.edu

Accommodations: The monastery accommodates 10 male guests in single rooms, each with a private bath.

Meals: Thee meals daily

Costs: $10 for room and $20 for meals, per person per day

Directions: From points east or west, take I-12 to US 190 North. From points north or south (New Orleans is one hour south), take US 190 to Covington. Past Covington, take LA 437 (Lee Rd.) East, then turn left on River Rd. Abbey will be on right.

Public Transportation: There is Greyhound bus service to Covington. Contact guest master for further information.

History: St. Joseph Abbey was founded in 1890 by monks from St. Meinrad Archabbey, Indiana. From the beginning their principal work has been their seminary. More recently their labors have been expanded to include retreats, a summer camp for boys and girls, and Pennies for Bread and the Abbey, a program that supplies abbey-baked bread to the area's poor and needy. St. Joseph is home to about 50 monks.

Description: On the banks of the Bogue Falaya River, the abbey's 1,200 acres include cultivated areas, and forests of pine and hardwoods. The abbey church is a massive Classical Revival building. The interior walls of the church and the monastic dining hall are covered with stunning murals painted over the course of a decade by the Belgian monk Dom Gregory de Wit.

Points of Interest: The abbey is 7 miles north of New Orleans and Lake Pontchartrain.

Special Note: In addition to accommodating men in the monastery, the abbey opens its doors to men and women at the Abbey Christian Life Center. Built in 1965, the center offers modest but comfortable rooms with private baths for groups of up to 41 persons.

✤ MAINE

Franciscan Monastery and Guest House

26 Beach Ave., Kennebunk Beach, ME 04043

Order: Franciscan Friars (Roman Catholic)

Contact: Front Desk

Telephone: 207-967-4865. **Best time to call:** 9 AM to 5 PM Eastern Time

Web site: www.franciscanguesthouse.com; **e-mail:** info@franciscan guesthouse.com

Accommodations: Houses up to 150 guests in single, twin, and multiple-occupancy rooms, each with private bath.

Meals: Three meals daily

Costs: Room rates vary according to season, from $69 to $159, plus 7 percent tax.

Directions: From points south, take I-95 to Wells (Exit 19). Take exit ramp to light. Turn left on ME 109 and drive 1.6 miles. Then make left at set of lights onto US 1 North for 1.8 miles, then right on ME 9 East for 4.2 miles to intersection of ME 9 and ME 35. Make right onto Beach Ave. Franciscan Monastery and Guest House will be on left.

Public Transportation: Contact reservations office for information.

History: Kennebunk is an Indian name. The first European to explore this area was Samuel de Champlain. That was in 1604. Three centuries later the Tudor-style house on this site was built and later was sold to Lithuanian Franciscans.

Description: The monastery grounds is a pleasant 60-acre park designed by the Olmstead Brothers, now dotted with statues, shrines, a grotto, the Stations of the Cross, and an outdoor sculpture commissioned for the Vatican Pavilion at the 1964–65 New York World's Fair.

Points of Interest: Probably the best-known spot in the Kennebunks is the summer home of President George H. W. Bush. The Seashore Trolley Museum, Rachel Carson National Wildlife Refuge, and the History Center of Kennebunkport also are nearby. The Kennebunks have a wide variety of shops, galleries, cafés, and restaurants. Guests may also wish to visit the local beaches, take a scenic cruise, or participate in a whale-watching excursion.

Special Note: The Intown Trolley stops at the guest house.

✤ MARYLAND

All Saints Convent

P.O. Box 3127, 1501 Hilton Ave., Catonsville, MD 21228

Order: All Saints Sisters of the Poor (Roman Catholic)

Contact: Guest Mistress

Telephone: 410-747-4104. Call between 10 AM and noon, between 2 PM and 3 PM, or between 3:30 PM and 4:45 PM Eastern Time

Web site: www.asspconvent.org

Accommodations: Convent houses eight women guests in single rooms, all with shared bath. Men seeking a nondirected individual retreat may be accommodated at St. Gabriel's Retreat House, also on convent grounds.

Meals: Three meals daily

Costs: Freewill offering

Directions: The convent is 10 miles south of Baltimore. Take I-95 and exit at Catonsville (Exit 47) to Rolling Rd. (MD 166). When Rolling Rd. meets Hilton Ave. make sharp left. Convent is at end of Hilton Ave.

Public Transportation: There is air service to Baltimore-Washington International Airport, and train service to BWI Airport Rail Station. Pickups can be arranged with prior notification.

History: Founded in London in 1851, the sisters were named for the parish they served: All Saints Margaret Street, a parish of the Church of England. In 1872 a group was sent to Baltimore to work among the city's poor, and in 1917 a gift was made of the Catonsville property. For more than a century the sisters have carried on a number of charitable projects including schools, a summer day-camp for inner-city children, a home for elderly women, care for the terminally ill, and retreat work. The All Saints Scriptorium is widely known, and greeting cards are sold at the Convent Card Shop and by mail order. Long a religious community in the Episcopal Church, the sisters were received into the Roman Catholic Church in September 2009.

Description: The beautiful fieldstone Gothic Revival chapel and convent are set on 90 acres of natural woodlands, all of which is surrounded by state parklands.

Point of Interest: The convent is contiguous with Patapsco Valley State Park, where there are several trails for walks and hikes.

Special Note: Group retreats for men and women are offered at St. Gabriel's Retreat House. For retreat schedules, contact the convent.

✤ MASSACHUSETTS

Adelynrood Retreat and Conference Center
46 Elm St., Byfield, MA 01922

Order: Society of the Companions of the Holy Cross (Episcopal)

Contact: Katheryn Ostertag, Assistant Manager

Telephone: 978-462-6721. Best times to call: May to Sept., daily 9 AM to 9 PM; Oct. to Apr., Mon. to Fri. 9 AM to 5 PM Eastern Time

Web site: www.adelynrood.org; **e-mail:** KathrynOstertag@Adelynrood.org

Accommodations: Main House accommodates up to 64 guests, in 40 single and 12 double rooms, all with shared baths. There are also three cabins with private baths for extended stays.

Meals: "Outstanding meals three times each day, gourmet quality and fresh produce."

Costs: $50 per person per night for a room only. Breakfast is $10, lunch is $20, and dinner is $20. Or for room and three meals, $100 per person per day. Scholarships are available.

Directions: Adelynrood is 40 miles north of Boston. From I-95 take Exit 55. Go east on Central St. in Byfield, then follow signs to Governor's Academy, which is next door to Adelynrood.

Public Transportation: C&J Trailways Bus has service from Logan Airport and Boston's South Station to Newburyport. Contact assistant manager in advance for further information.

History: Adelynrood, begun by the Society of the Companions of the Holy Cross in 1901, is believed to be the oldest continuously operated retreat in the country. One early member of the society was Adelyn Henry Howard. She lived in Hartford, Connecticut, and died of tuberculosis at the age of 32. Her name was added to "rood" (Early English for "cross") and formed Adelynrood. The society, founded in 1884, now numbers about 700 women throughout the Anglican Communion.

Description: Built in 1914, the main house has public rooms, libraries, and a long screened porch. The 14-acre property has gardens, pine trees, and trails.

Points of Interest: The Governor's Academy prep school (founded 1763) is next door. Nearby there are a number of historic and scenic towns including Newburyport, West Newbury, and Ipswich. Parker River National Wildlife Refuge, Plum Island Wildlife Refuge and beaches, and Joppa Flats Education Center are close by and provide excellent vantage points for nature and bird watching.

Special Note: Guests may participate in Adelynrood's daily Holy Routine if they wish.

Beacon Hill Friends House

6 Chestnut St., Boston, MA 02108

Order: Society of Friends/Quakers

Contact: Residency Manager

Telephone: 617-227-9118. **Best time to call:** Mon. through Fri. 9 AM to 5 PM Eastern Time

Web site: www.bhfh.org; **e-mail:** directors@bhfh.org

Accommodations: Two guest rooms with shared bath accommodate up to seven guests.

Meals: Three meals daily. Breakfast and lunch are self-prepared. Dinner is prepared by the staff and is vegetarian Sun. through Thurs.

Costs: Room rates vary from $75–$90 for single occupancy to $110 for a room with four guests. Breakfast is included. Lunch is $4.50 and dinner is $7.50.

Directions: From points north or south, take I-93 to the Leverett Circle/Storrow Dr./Cambridge exit. Exit left at Charles Circle. At third light on Charles St. turn left on Mount Vernon St. and drive up hill to the "Do Not Enter" signs. Turn right on Walnut St. and take next right onto Chestnut St. The house will be on left. Parking is available at Boston Common Garage.

Public Transportation: Take the T (subway) Red Line to the Charles/MGH Station. Walk down Charles St. to Chestnut St. and turn left.

History: The Beacon Hill Friends House was opened as a residence for college students in 1957. Its directors encouraged diversity by admitting many foreign students. "The house started with the intention of living out Quaker values and educating non-Quakers about Quakerism. We currently have residents aging 18–mid 60s, of all different faiths and non-faiths."

Description: Originally two town houses, Beacon Hill Friends House, designed by one of America's most notable architects, Charles Bulfinch, was built in 1804. The two houses were joined in the 1920s. In addition to the guest rooms there are a library, parlor, music room, lounge, meeting room, dining room, kitchen, two courtyards, and a deck.

Points of Interest: Beacon Hill is in the heart of old Boston. On one side of the hill are the Boston Common (1640), Boston Public Garden (1839), and the Massachusetts State House (1795, another Bulfinch design), and on the opposite side is the Esplanade walk along the shores of the Charles River.

Special Note: Christy Little, the residency manager, states that "guests share living space with 21 residents . . . We have a laid-back hospitality that expects guests to serve themselves. We also want to make you comfortable, and you can ask anyone around if you have questions."

> *Ye are the light of the world. A city that is set on an hill cannot be hid.*
>
> —MATTHEW 5:14

> *For we must consider that we shall be as a city upon a hill.*
>
> —JOHN WINTHROP (1588–1649),
> FIRST GOVERNOR OF
> MASSACHUSETTS BAY COLONY

Glastonbury Abbey

16 Hull St., Hingham, MA 02043

Order: Benedictine Monks (Roman Catholic)

Contact: Retreat Secretary

Telephone: 781-749-2155, ext. 200. **Best time to call:** Mon. through Fri. 8 AM to 1 PM Eastern Time

Web site: www.glastonburyabbey.org; **e-mail:** retreats@glastonbury abbey.org

Accommodations: Two guest houses serve up to 31 individuals, in 23 rooms (single and twin), some of which have private baths.

Meals: Three meals daily

Costs: Suggested minimum offering of $60 to $70 per night for room and meals

Directions: From Boston, take I-93 South (Southeast Expressway) to MA 3 South (toward Cape Cod) to Exit 14 (Route 228, Rockland-Hingham). Follow Route 228 North (Main St., Hingham) about 7 miles to abbey.

From New York, Connecticut, or Rhode Island, take I-95 to I-93 North to MA 3 South (toward Cape Cod). Take Exit 14 as above.

From Massachusetts Turnpike (I-90) exit at I-95 South. This road becomes I-93 North. Follow I-93 to MA 3 South (toward Cape Cod). Take Exit 14 as above.

Public Transportation: Take the MBTA commuter rail (Purple Line) from Boston's South Station to the Cohasset Station. Arrange in advance to be picked up at Cohasset by someone from abbey. The Cohasset Station is less than 1 mile from abbey.

History: At the invitation of Cardinal Cushing, monks from Benet Lake, Wisconsin, arrived here in 1954, founding this, the first Benedictine monastery in Massachusetts.

Description: Less than 2 miles from the Atlantic Ocean, the abbey owns 60 wooded acres. The guest houses, Stonecrest and Whiting House, have the appearance of attractive and comfortable homes.

Points of Interest: Historic Hingham, 16 miles south of Boston, was founded in 1635. The Old Ship Church (1681) in Hingham is the last remaining Puritan meetinghouse in America.

Special Note: In addition to extending hospitality to individual guests, the abbey has a full schedule of group retreats. A calendar and further information are available from the retreat secretary.

Monastery of St. Mary and St. John
980 Memorial Dr., Cambridge, MA 02138

Order: Society of St. John the Evangelist (Episcopal)

Contact: Guest House Manager

Telephone: 617-876-3037

Web site: www.ssje.org; **e-mail:** guesthouse@ssje.org

Accommodations: Guest house welcomes up to 14 individuals in single rooms. Each room has its own sink; toilets and showers are nearby.

Meals: Three meals daily

Costs: Suggested donation of $50 per person per day for room and meals. Guests may register by telephone or online. Deposits and full payment may be made by check or credit card (Mastercard or Visa).

Directions: From Route 128, take Route 2 East. Make left onto Memorial Dr. Monastery will be on left. Contact guest house manager in advance for parking directions.

Public Transportation: Take T (subway) Red Line to Harvard Square. Walk down J. F. Kennedy St. to Memorial Dr. Make right on Memorial; monastery will be on right just past Harvard's Kennedy School of Government.

History: The Society of St. John the Evangelist, the oldest monastic community in the Anglican Communion, was founded in 1866 in the village of Cowley St. John near Oxford, England. For that reason, members of the Society in the past were popularly known as the Cowley Fathers. In 1870 the fathers came to Boston, later settling their American motherhouse across the Charles River in Cambridge. The community presently includes lay and ordained brothers engaged in the ministries of preaching, teaching, and spiritual direction.

Description: The monastery was designed by architect Ralph Adams Cram, whose best-known work is the nave of the Cathedral of St. John the Divine in New York City. The granite church is Romanesque. The church, guest house, and monastery are all contiguous, surrounding a small garden. Guests are free to walk along the banks of the Charles River just across Memorial Drive and to enjoy the views of Harvard's Georgian towers and of Boston in the distance.

Points of Interest: The monastery is virtually on the doorstep of Harvard University, and the T (subway) in Harvard Square provides easy access to the sights of Boston.

Special Note: The guest house is "primarily for those making retreats in prayer and quiet." Depending on the length of the retreat that is booked, guests may arrive from Tuesday through Friday. Guests may not arrive on Saturday, Sunday, or Monday. Unless other arrangements are made, arrival times are between 10 AM to noon, or between 2 PM and 4 PM. All guests leave by Sunday afternoon, which is the start of the brothers' Sabbath.

Mount St. Mary's Abbey

300 Arnold St., Wrentham, MA 02093

Order: Cistercian (Trappistine) Nuns (Roman Catholic)

Contact: Guest Sister

Telephone: 508-528-1282. **Best time to call:** 9 AM to 5 PM Eastern Time

Web site: www.msmabbey.org; **e-mail:** hospitality@msmabbey.org

Accommodations: The abbey accommodates up to five guests in an apartment, two single rooms, and one twin-bedded room, each with private bath. In the guest house there are 14 single rooms, all with shared baths.

Meals: Three meals a day ("basic foods only")

Costs: Donation of $40 per person per day for room and meals

Directions: From points north or south take I-95 to I-495 North to Wrentham. Contact the guest sister for further directions.

Public Transportation: Contact the guest sister for information.

History: In 1949 sisters from Glencairn, Ireland, founded this, the first Trappistine monastery in America. Mount St. Mary's has, in turn, founded other monasteries in the states. The abbey church, renovated in 1998, is a gathering place for prayer for the abbey's 48 nuns. They support themselves through work on their farm and the production and sale of Trappistine Quality Candy.

St. Benedict Abbey

252 Still River Rd., Still River, MA 01467

Order: Benedictine Monks (Roman Catholic)

Contact: Guest Master

Telephone: 978-456-3221

Web site: www.abbey.org; **e-mail:** abbeyretreats@aol.com

Accommodations: Guest house accommodates up to 60 individuals, in single and twin-bedded rooms, some with private bath.

Meals: Three meals daily

Costs: $35 per person per day for room and meals

Directions: From Boston area, take Route 2 West to Route 110/111 toward town of Harvard. From south, west, or north, take I-495 to Route 117 West to Route 110 (Still River Rd.).

Public Transportation: From Boston's North Station take MBTA commuter rail (Purple Line) to Ayer, Massachusetts. Arrange in advance with the guest master for pickup on arrival; alternately, there is taxi service from Ayer.

Description: The abbey is situated on 70 acres of woodlands and fields overlooking Mount Wachusett and the Nashoba Valley. Several colonial homes form the nucleus of the abbey. The monks' house dates to 1683 and has paintings and chairs of the period. The chapel is a former carriage house in which the traditional Latin Gregorian chant is sung. The 250-year-old guest house is available to individual guests, families, and groups. In addition to bedrooms, it has several living rooms, a conference room, a library, and a small chapel.

Points of Interest: Historic Lexington and Concord are near the abbey, as is Fruitlands Museum. Fruitlands is the remains of an 18th-century Utopian Transcendental community, which, like the abbey, overlooks the valley.

St. Joseph's Abbey

167 North Spencer Rd., Spencer, MA 01562

Order: Cistercian (Trappist) Monks (Roman Catholic)

Contact: Guest Master

Telephone: 508-885-8710. Call: between 9 AM and 11 AM or between 1:30 PM and 5 PM Eastern Time

Web site: www.spencerabbey.org

Accommodations: Retreat house accommodates 11 men, each in a single room with private bath. Women are accommodated exclusively in the retreat house the third week of each month and the weekend following. See Special Note below.

Meals: Three meals daily

Costs: Freewill offerings, but the average minimum is about $100–$200 for a weekend and $200–$400 for a midweek retreat.

Directions: The abbey is in central Massachusetts. From east or west, take the Massachusetts Turnpike (I-90) to Exit 10 (Auburn). Then go west on Route 12 and US 20 for 3 miles. Go right on Route 56 to Leister (8 miles), then left on Route 9 to Spencer (9 miles). From Route 9 make right onto Route 31 to abbey (5 miles).

From the south, take I-84 East to Exit 3A (Sturbridge/US 20 East). Go 2 miles to Route 49 North (8 miles to Spencer). Then take Route 9 East to Route 31 North in center of town. Abbey is on left in 5 miles.

Public Transportation: Amtrak, Greyhound, and Peter Pan offer service to Worcester, and there is an airport there as well. There is taxi service to the abbey from Worcester and the airport; ask for a flat rate. Or take the Worcester Regional Transit Authority #33 bus to center of Spencer; there is no public transportation from there to the abbey. Contact guest master for additional information.

History: With roots in 12th-century French and Belgian monasteries, this community began in Nova Scotia in 1825, moved to Rhode Island in 1900, and to Spencer in 1950. The fieldstones for the abbey building were hauled from the surrounding farmland. Under the supervision of an architect and contractor the monks built their abbey in 1952–53. Today the monks support themselves through the production and sale of Trappist Preserves and the design and creation of liturgical vestments at the Holy Rood Guild.

Description: The abbey property includes nearly 2,000 acres of woodland and cultivated fields. The retreat house is attached to the monastery and church where the monks sing services daily in Gregorian chant (in English).

Special Note: A weekend retreat begins on Friday afternoon and ends on Sunday after lunch. The midweek retreat extends from Monday afternoon until Friday morning. One conference is given each day. Reservations should be made six months in advance.

About 0.25 mile from the abbey entrance is the Mary House, an independently run four-bedroom retreat open to men and women. For more information contact the Mary House at P.O. Box 20, Spencer, MA 01562 (call 508-885-5450, or visit www.maryhousema.com).

> *The eleventh degree of humility is, that when a monk speaketh, he do so gently and without laughter, humbly, gravely, with few and reasonable words, and that he be not noisy in his speech, as it is written: "A wise man is known by the fewness of his words."*
>
> —RULE OF SAINT BENEDICT

St. Margaret's Convent

17 Highland Park St., Boston, MA 02119

Order: Society of St. Margaret (Episcopal)

Contact: Reservations Office

Telephone: 617-445-8961, ext 127

Web site: www.ssmbos.org; **e-mail:** reservations@ssmbos.org

Accommodations: The convent houses up to 17 guests, most in single rooms and most with shared baths. Handicap-accessible rooms are available. In addition, the Carriage House accommodates four guests in two twin-bedded rooms in a spacious second-floor apartment. There is also a double futon in the living area. The apartment has a kitchen where light meals may be prepared.

Meals: For those staying in the convent, three meals are served daily. Meals are self-prepared by those staying in the Carriage House, where continental breakfast items are supplied.

Costs: $65 per person per night for room and meals for those staying in the convent; $90 per person per night for bed and breakfast for those staying in the Carriage House. Group rates are available. A 50 percent deposit is required to confirm reservations.

Directions: Contact reservations office for driving directions.

Public Transportation: Take the T (MBTA subway) Orange Line to Roxbury Crossing station. Contact reservations office for further information.

History: The Society of St. Margaret was founded in England in 1855 by John Mason Neale (priest, hymnologist, and author). In 1873 the Society came to Boston to supervise nurses at the Children's Hospital and later extended its ministry to other areas. This five-acre property, site of the former home of the great abolitionist William Lloyd Garrison, was acquired by the sisters in 1907. The Society administered St. Monica's Home here for many years. In 1989 it was decided to move the convent from Louisburg Square on Beacon Hill to this property.

Description: St. Margaret's Convent is on a rocky hill in Roxbury, 3 miles from downtown Boston. The convent is a modern, light-filled, cheerful, and energy-efficient facility. It is in a convenient location and yet removed from the noise and congestion of the city.

Point of Interest: The city of Boston, with its many historic and cultural attractions, is easily accessible from the convent.

Special Notes: Those staying in the convent have a curfew of 9 PM; those staying in the Carriage House do not have a curfew.

In addition to serving individual guests, the convent welcomes groups at its DeBlois Conference Center. There, groups of up to 21 may be accommodated overnight; the center can accommodate groups of up to 40 for day use.

St. Margaret's Convent
Harden Hill Rd., Duxbury, MA 02332-5115

Order: Society of St. Margaret (Episcopal)

Contact: Reservations Office

Telephone: 617-445-8961, ext. 127

Web site: www.ssmbos.org; **e-mail:** reservations@ssmbos.org

Accommodations: There are three places for guests to stay at St. Margaret's. The first is the Boathouse. An ideal spot for a summer vacation, the Boathouse is open from June to October. The second is the Farmhouse, which predates the American Revolution. It has recently been restored. And finally there is the Bertram Conference Center. Contact the reservations office for specific information regarding these accommodations.

Meals: Contact the reservations office regarding meals.

Costs: Fees are variable according to the season. Contact the reservations office for information.

Directions: From Boston area, take the Southeast Expressway (Route 3) South to Exit 10. Follow Route 3A North about 1 mile to blinking light. Turn right and follow signs to South Duxbury. At flagpole, cross over, leaving the liquor store on your right and the Exxon gas station on your left. You will be on Washington St. After about 0.25 mile, Harden Hill Rd. will be on right.

Public Transportation: From Boston, the Plymouth & Brockton Bus Line has service to its terminal in Plymouth. Contact reservations office for further information.

History: The town of Duxbury was founded by settlers from Plymouth, perhaps as early as 1628. Before the American Revolution it was mainly a farming community. Following the Revolution, the fishing and ship-building industries prospered during the golden age of shipbuilding in the period between the War of 1812 and the Civil War. The Society acquired this site in 1904 to be used as a refuge from hot Boston summers.

Description: Both the Boathouse and the Farmhouse have living rooms with working fireplaces. Guests enjoy beautiful views of Duxbury Bay from the porches and from most bedroom windows, and the smell of fresh salt air. There are several beautifully landscaped acres for walks and a private beach.

Points of Interest: Duxbury is a very old and quaint residential town. It is a 20-minute car ride from Duxbury to Plymouth. There, Plymouth Rock, *Mayflower II*, and the reconstructed Plimoth Plantation may be visited.

St. Scholastica Priory and St. Mary's Monastery

P.O. Box 345, 271 N. Main St., Petersham, MA 01366-0345

Order: Benedictine Monks and Nuns (Roman Catholic)

Contacts: Women: Guest Mistress; Men: Guest Master

Telephone: Women: 978-724-3213 (or 3217); Men: 978-724-3350

Web sites: www.stscholaticapriory.org; www.stmarysmonastery.org; **e-mails:** Women: guestmistress@aol.com; Men: monks@stmarysmona stery.org

Accommodations: Guest house accommodates up to 18, in twelve single and three double rooms, all with shared baths.

Meals: Three meals daily. The main meal is at midday.

Costs: "Freewill"

Directions: From Boston, take Route 2 West to Athol/Petersham Exit 17 (Route 32). Turn right at bottom of ramp onto Route 32 South and go about 3.5 miles. Priory and monastery are on right after Harvard University Forest and before Petersham Country Club.

Public Transportation: There is bus service from Boston's South Station to Gardner, Massachusetts. One of the monks or nuns can meet you on arrival if prior arrangement has been made.

History: St. Scholastica Priory is a community of nuns, and St. Mary's Monastery is a community of monks affiliated with Pluscarden Abbey in Scotland. Both communities live a contemplative life and share the church, where the services are sung in Gregorian chant in Latin with some English. The guest house is also shared by both communities.

Description: The monastic buildings consist of a central large church, with an adjoining building on one side for the nuns, and another on the other side for the monks. The guest house is a separate building a short distance away. All are on a secluded 185-acre wooded property.

Points of Interest: The Harvard University Forest, just across the road from the priory and monastery, has marked trails and a nature museum. Also close by is the Quabbin Reservoir, which covers 128 square miles and offers opportunities for scenic drives, hiking, and fishing. Petersham is close to Massachusetts' historic Pioneer Valley and the Five Colleges area of Amherst and Northampton.

✤ MICHIGAN

St. Augustine's House
P.O. Box 125, 3316 E. Drahner Rd., Oxford, MI 48371

Order: Congregation of the Servants of Christ/Benedictine Monks (Lutheran)

Contact: Prior

Telephone: 248-628-5155 (office) and 248-628-2604 (guest house)

Web site: www.staugustineshouse.org; **e-mail:** staughouse@aol.com

Accommodations: Guest house accommodates six men in single rooms, all with shared bath. There are also limited accommodations for one or two women.

Meals: Three meals daily. Lighter fare on ordinary Wednesdays and Fridays.

Costs: Suggested donation of $30 to $35 per person per day for room and meals.

Directions: From the south (Detroit), take I-75 North to Pontiac. Exit onto M-24 (Exit 81). Continue north on M-24 to Oxford and turn east (right) onto E. Drahner Rd. St. Augustine's House is 2.5 miles east on north side of E. Drahner Rd.

From the north (Flint, Lapeer), take M-24 South and turn left onto E. Drahner Rd.

Public Transportation: From Detroit Metropolitan Airport there is limousine service to Pontiac. There is also bus and train service to Pontiac, and train service to Lapeer.

History: This, the only Lutheran monastery in the United States, was founded in 1958 by the Reverend Arthur Carl Kreinheder, a priest of the Church of Sweden. Following World War II there was a rekindled interest in monastic life among Lutherans and other Christians, especially in Europe. This community is an outgrowth of that movement. It follows the Rule of Saint Benedict. Though affiliated with the Evangelical Lutheran Church in America, St. Augustine's House serves a diverse family of associate members and retreatants: Lutherans, Roman Catholics, Episcopalians, Orthodox Chistians, and many others.

Description: The community owns 42 acres of hilly, wooded land in a rural setting. Six buildings are on the monastery grounds. The retreat house stands on a hilltop and has a beautiful view, which in winter extends for miles. The Church of the Visitation of the Blessed Virgin Mary, built in 2001, is "splendidly simple and focused for prayer and meditation." More recently (2008) a new monastery building was completed.

Special Note: Guest information and maps are available on request.

St. Gregory's Abbey

56500 Abbey Rd., Three Rivers, MI 49093

Order: Benedictine Monks (Episcopal)

Contact: Guest Master

Telephone: 616-244-5893

Web site: www.saintgregorysthreerivers.org; **e-mail:** guestmaster@saintgregorysthreerivers.org

Accommodations: St. Anthony's Guest House can serve four guests in single rooms. There are also accommodations for five guests in single rooms in St. Denys Guest House. There are shared baths at each facility. Families or groups may be accommodated at St. Benedict's Guest Cottage.

Meals: Three meals daily for those staying at St. Anthony's. Meals are self-prepared by guests staying at St. Denys and St. Benedict's.

Costs: Freewill offerings accepted

Directions: Take US 131 to Three Rivers. In northern part of city you will come to Hoffman Rd. (at a traffic light). Go west on Hoffman about 4 miles until you come to Abbey Rd. on right (road on left has different name). Look for St. Gregory's Abbey sign. Turn right onto Abbey Rd. St. Gregory's is on left in about 1 mile. Guest parking lot is identified with a wood-and-brick St. Gregory's Abbey sign.

Public Transportation: There is air, train, and bus service to Kalamazoo. With prior arrangement, a monk may meet you on arrival, except on Sundays and major holy days.

History: The Anglican Benedictine monks of Nashdom Abbey, England, founded an American branch in 1939 in Indiana. The monks moved to Three Rivers in 1946, and in 1969 St. Gregory's Priory was raised to the status of a fully independent abbey.

Description: The abbey, its church, monastery, guest houses, and other buildings are in a park-like setting surrounded by woods and farmland.

Special Note: Reservations should be made as far in advance as possible. The normal length of stay is from two days to one week. Weekend retreats for groups are scheduled from August through June. For an update, brochures, and further information, contact the guest master. The community invites all guests to participate in daily Mass and sevenfold Divine Office, all of which are said or sung in English.

❖ MINNESOTA

Skete of the Resurrection of Christ

1201 Hathaway Ln., Fridley, MN 55432

Order: Monks (Synod of Bishops of the Russian Orthodox Church Outside Russia)

Contact: Father Abbot

Telephone: 612-574-1001

Web site: www.skete.info; **e-mail:** rusmnch@worldnet.att.net

Accommodations: Monastery can serve two guests in single rooms, both with shared bath.

Meals: One complete meal served daily

Costs: $50 per person per day for room and meal

Directions: From I-694 take Exit 38 and turn north on Central Ave./CR 65. Stay in right lane; turn right onto Central Ave. NE. Make an immediate right onto Hackman St., and right again on Hathaway Ln.

Public Transportation: Take MetroTransit bus #10M or #10N to Moore Lake.

History: A skete is a small community of monks, and in 1989 this small but growing community acquired its present home on the outskirts of Minneapolis.

Description: With imagination and hard work the monks (and parishioners of the Church of the Resurrection of Christ) have transformed a suburban house into an inviting and functional monastery. The heart of the skete is the Chapel of St. Seraphim. The icon screen in the chapel is old, having once stood in a cathedral. The traditional iconography, the chants in Old Church Slavonic and English, the incense and vestments, all combine to create an intimate shrine with perhaps one of the finest expressions of Russian Orthodox liturgy outside Russia.

Points of Interest: The skete is 15 minutes from downtown Minneapolis and its parks, lakes, museums, and the IDS Center.

Special Note: Please contact the skete for reservations one month in advance.

> *Christ is risen from the dead,*
> *Trampling on death by death,*
> *And on those in the tombs,*
> *Bestowing life.*
>
> —HYMN FOR EASTER, DIVINE LITURGY
> OF SAINT JOHN CHRYSOSTOM

St. John's Abbey

P.O. Box 2015, 31802 County Rd. 159, Collegeville, MN 56321-2015

Order: Benedictine Monks (Roman Catholic)

Contact: Guest Master

Telephone: 320-363-2573

Web site: www.saintjohnsabbey.org; **e-mail:** guestmaster@osb.org

Accommodations: Houses up to 44 guests in 14 single and 15 double rooms, each with private bath.

Meals: Thee meals daily

Costs: Rooms are $65 per day, single occupancy, and $85 per day, double occupancy. Meals are $18 per person per day.

Directions: From Minneapolis (80 miles away), take I-94 West to Exit 156.

Public Transportation: Executive Express (888-522-9899) offers commuter service from the Minneapolis–St. Paul International Airport directly to the abbey. Call in advance.

History: Five monks from St. Vincent's Archabbey (Pennsylvania) came to the Minnesota Territory in 1856, shortly after it was opened for settlement. Their primary missions were to work with the German immigrants in the area and to open a school for children. Like many of their fellow pioneers, the first monks lived in log cabins. In time, they made a permanent foundation in what is now called Collegeville, a beautiful wooded area between the Watab Creek and Lake Sagatagan. St. John's University was chartered by the territorial legislature in 1857. The campus is also the site of a prep school, the Liturgical Press, the Institute for Ecumenical and Cultural Research, KSJR-FM (founding station of Minnesota Public Radio), and the Hill Museum and Manuscript Library. The abbey numbers more than 150 monks today.

Description: St. John's has nearly 2,500 acres of land, of which 1,500 acres are forested with 24 species of hardwoods. In 1988 the abbey embarked on a major environmental project: the restoration of 135 acres to their original natural state. This includes a 60-acre wetland, home to more than 90 species of waterfowl, songbirds, and furbearers. Furthermore, in 1990, 50 acres were returned to their prairie state with more than 100 species of grass and wildflowers. No description of St. John's would be complete without mentioning the Abbey and University Church designed by Marcel Breuer. A "bell banner" marks the church's entrance. Once inside, one becomes aware of the nave's monumental grandeur—225 feet in length, with a breadth of 180 feet.

We have, therefore, to establish a school of the Lord's service, in the setting forth of which we hope to order nothing that is harsh or rigorous.

—RULE OF SAINT BENEDICT

❖ MISSISSIPPI

St. Augustine's Retreat Center

210 N. Second St., Bay St. Louis, MS 39520

Order: Divine Word Missionaries (Roman Catholic)

Contact: Coordinator

Telephone: 228-467-2032

E-mail: awallssvd@yahoo.com

Accommodations: Houses up to 40 persons in single, twin, and multiple-occupancy rooms, each with its own bath. In addition, Fr. Wendell Hall has ten smaller single rooms and a suite, each with its own bath.

Meals: Three meals daily

Costs: $30–$60 per night, depending on location and meals

Directions: Bay St. Louis is about 50 miles east of New Orleans. From New Orleans or Slidell, Louisiana, take I-10 East. Get off at first exit in Mississippi (MS 607). Continue east on US 90 to Bay St. Louis. Turn right on N. Second St. (first right after highway shrine on seminary grounds). Turn right to retreat center (i.e., second right turn possible after US 90).

From points east, take US 90 from Gulfport and cross Bay St. Louis Bridge. Turn left on North Second St. (i.e., second left turn possible after bridge). Turn right into retreat center (second right turn possible after US 90).

Public Transportation: There is air service to Gulfport-Biloxi Regional Airport and New Orleans International Airport. Greyhound has bus service to Bay St. Louis. Contact coordinator for further information.

History: St. Augustine's Retreat Center is a ministry of the Divine Word Missionaries, a society of priests and brothers founded in 1875. St. Augustine's, which dates to the 1920s, has the distinction of being the first Roman Catholic seminary in the United States opened for the education and training of African American youth in the society. Though St. Augustine's has always been a place of retreat, the retreat center began as a full-time ministry in 1982. It suffered extensive damage during Hurricane Katrina in 2005. Rebuilt, the center was reopened in October 2008. It is fully air-conditioned.

Description: St. Augustine's is best described as "a prayerful, peaceful, and reflective" place with views of the Mississippi Sound and the Gulf Islands National Seashore. The property has shrines, grottoes, lawns, and trees such as palms, dogwoods, and ancient tall oaks draped with Spanish moss.

Points of Interest: US 90 provides a scenic drive along the Gulf of Mexico to New Orleans. In the Vieux Carré (French Quarter) is St. Louis Cathedral (1794).

Special Note: St. Augustine's welcomes "lay people, clergy and religious, single persons and married couples, all ages" with "warm Southern hospitality!"

❖ MISSOURI

Assumption Abbey

P.O. Box 1056, Route 5, Ava, MO 65608-9142

Order: Cistercian (Trappist) Monks (Roman Catholic)

Contact: Guest Master

Telephone: 417-683-5110. Best times to call: 9 AM to 11:30 AM and 1 PM to 4:30 PM Central Time

Web site: www.assumptionabbey.org; **e-mail:** avaguesthouse@hughes.net

Accommodations: Monastery guest wing houses up to 9 guests in single rooms, with one bath for every two rooms.

Meals: Three meals daily

Costs: Freewill offering

Directions: From St. Louis take I-44 West to Rolla. Take US 63 South to US 60 at Cabool. Go west on US 60 to Route C at Norwood. Drive south on Route C to Route 14. Drive east on Route 14 for 0.125 mile to Assumption Abbey sign on right marking CR 335. Abbey will be on left in 5 miles.

Public Transportation: Contact guest master for best options.

History: In 1950 monks from New Melleray Abbey, Iowa, came to Missouri and founded Assumption Abbey. To support themselves during their first decade in their new home, the monks farmed and tended orchards and vineyards. In the 1960s, using sand and gravel from their land, they began to make concrete blocks. This proved to be a successful industry. Concrete blocks were used in the construction of the monastery in 1970. Since the mid-1980s the monks have turned their labors to baking fruit-cakes, an industry that they find "suits our monastic rhythm well."

Description: Set amid crystal streams and rugged cliffs, the abbey is "an oasis of prayer, peace, and solitude."

Conception Abbey

P.O. Box 501, 37174 State Highway VV, Conception, MO 64433

Order: Benedictine Monks (Roman Catholic)

Contact: Director

Telephone: 660-944-2809 or 2909. **Best time to call:** 8 AM to 4:30 PM Central Time

Web site: www.conceptionabbey.org; **e-mail:** guests@conception.edu

Accommodations: Abbey Guest House accommodates up to 200 individuals, most in double rooms and all with shared baths.

Meals: Three meals daily

Costs: Suggested donation of $50 per person per day for single room and meals, or three days and two nights for $100. In a double-occupancy room the suggested donation is $85 per couple per night, or $170 for three days and two nights. For a suite, add an additional $25.

Directions: The abbey is 90 miles from Kansas City. Take I-29 North to US 71 North toward Maryville to Route M. Turn east (right) on Route M, continuing about 7 miles to Route AH. Turn north (left) on Route AH, continuing 5 miles to Highway W. Turn east (right) on Highway W. Drive 1 mile to abbey entrance.

Public Transportation: There is no public transportation to abbey.

History: In 1873 two monks from Engelberg Abbey near Lucerne, Switzerland, founded what later became Conception Abbey. The following year Conception College opened. The monks and local German and Irish immigrants built a monastery in 1881. The abbey church basilica was completed 10 years later. The Printery House was opened in the 1930s and now sells more than 5 million greeting cards annually and stocks more than 1,000 products. Since the 1870s the monks have served local parishes and, until 1995, worked as missionaries on the Indian reservations of South Dakota. There are about 75 monks, some of whom work on the abbey grounds, farmland, and orchards, while others are teachers, writers, scholars, historians, artisans, or musicians.

Description: The guest house, monastery, and venerable basilica are surrounded by acres of farmland and countryside that guests may explore on walking trails, enjoying the sight of deer, birds, and other creatures along the way.

Queen of Heaven Solitude

12494 Highway T, Marionville, MO 65705

Order: Society of Our Mother of Peace (Roman Catholic)

Contact: Retreat Directress

Telephone: 417-744-2011. **Best time to call:** 9:30 AM to 3 PM Central Time

Accommodations: The Solitude has five single-occupancy cabin hermitages.

Meals: Three meals daily

Costs: "Offering according to means"

Directions: From St. Louis, take I-44 West, passing all Springfield exits. Take Exit 58, marked "02." After exiting, take Highway O (to right), which takes you past a gas station and a motel. After about 5 miles, Highway O intersects with Highway 174. Continue straight, noting that Highway O is thereafter T. After 2 miles on T, the Solitude's mailbox will be on right, with entrance on left. Contact retreat directress for a map and additional directions.

Public Transportation: There is air and Greyhound bus service to Springfield, Missouri. Arrange in advance for pickup on arrival.

History: The Society of Our Mother of Peace was begun in 1966. There is also a Solitude in High Ridge, Missouri.

Description: The Solitude is in a quiet farming area. The property is heavily wooded, and the retreat hermitages are in the woods, each about 100 yards from the other. There are also walking trails, a chapel, and a library, all for the use of guests.

Point of Interest: Branson, Missouri, known for its wide variety of attractions, is little more than an hour's drive from Marionville.

Special Note: "Our facilities are designed to provide silence and solitude for persons wishing to make a private retreat. Please note that the Solitude is open to visitors year round except Holy Week and December 20–27."

> *O Queen of Heaven, be joyful, alleluia,*
> *Because He whom so meekly thou bearest, alleluia,*
> *Hath arisen as he promised, alleluia.*
>
> —EASTERTIDE HYMN

Vision of Peace Hermitages

P.O. Box 69, 1000 Abbey Ln., Pevely, MO 06370

Order: Roman Catholic

Contact: Resident Director

Telephone: 636-475-3697. **Best time to call:** 9 AM to 5 PM Central Time

Web site: www.visionofpeacehermitages.org; **e-mail:** visofpeace@juno.com

Accommodations: There are eight single-occupancy hermitages. Each hermitage has its own bath and kitchen; linens and cooking utensils included. One hermitage is handicap accessible.

Meals: Guests provide their own food.

Costs: Suggested donation of $35 per night

Directions: Vision of Peace is 30 miles south of St. Louis and 2.5 miles east of I-55. From St. Louis, take I-55 to Exit 180 (Pevely/Hillsboro, Highway Z). Turn east on Highway Z and cross US 61/67. Continue 1 mile. Turn right (before "Vision of Peace" sign). Go 0.5 mile and park in gravel lot.

Public Transportation: There is no public transportation to Vision of Peace.

History: Originally known as Christina House Hermitages, this has been a place of retreat since 1977.

Description: Vision of Peace is a village of hermitages along the banks of the Mississippi River. Views of the river and the Illinois bluffs may be enjoyed from several vantage points on the property. In addition to the hermitages, Vision of Peace has a library with a collection of books, periodicals, tapes, and CDs.

Special Note: Vision of Peace offers daily services, spiritual direction, and directed retreats. Retreatants may attend Mass at the local parish church.

✤ NEBRASKA

Christ the King Priory
St. Benedict Center

P.O. Box 528, 1126 Road I, Schuyler, NE 68661

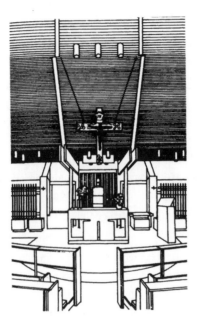

Order: Benedictine Monks (Roman Catholic)

Contact: Administrator

Telephone: 402-352-8819

Web site: www.stbenedictcenter.com; **e-mail:** retreats@stbenedictcenter
.com

Accommodations: St. Benedict Center houses up to 100 guests in 60 rooms, the majority of which are twin-bedded. Each room has a private bath. There are also two suites for retreat masters/directors. The center is fully air-conditioned.

Meals: Three meals daily

Costs: $61.75 per person per day for room and meals, single occupancy; $54.75 per person per day, double occupancy

Directions: From Omaha, take US 275 West to Fremont, then US 30 West to the NE 15/Schuyler exit on right. At stop sign, turn right onto NE 15 and go 3 miles north. At welcome sign at top of hill turn right. Take first left and drive around to parking area.

Public Transportation: There is air service to Omaha (65 miles west). Contact administrator for further information.

History: The Missionary Benedictine Congregation of St. Ottilien was founded in Germany in the late 19th century. Fearing the worst, a group of monks left Germany in the 1930s and settled in Nebraska, living more than 40 years in the Mission House, an old wood-frame farmhouse. The house served as the development and education office for the congregation's missions in Africa, Asia, and South America. A strikingly modern monastery was completed in 1979, and in 1997 St. Benedict Center, an ecumenical retreat and conference center offering peace, tranquility, and hospitality, was opened.

Description: The priory is unique in that it is literally set into the natural landscape, its roof and outer walls covered by a verdant carpet of grass. St. Benedict Center has a large chapel, meeting rooms, dining rooms, a solarium with library, a spacious lobby, and a gift shop selling a large selection of Christian art, books, and items from mission countries. A permanent exhibit provides a history of the congregation, displaying artifacts from various countries. Guests enjoy walks through the park and by the lake. Both the priory and center are surrounded by farmland.

Points of Interest: Omaha is the home of the Durham Museum and the Joslyn Art Museum. Father Flanagan's Boys Town is just west of Omaha, and the Strategic Air & Space Museum is in Ashland, about 20 miles southwest of Omaha.

❖ NEW HAMPSHIRE

St. Anselm Abbey

100 St. Anselm Dr., Manchester, NH 03102

Order: Benedictine Monks (Roman Catholic)

Contact: Guest Master

Telephone: 603-641-7277

Web site: www.anselm.edu; **e-mail:** bcamera@anselm.edu

Accommodations: Monastery accommodates male guests only, each in a single room with private bath.

Meals: Three meals daily

Costs: "There is no charge for staying here."

Directions: From points southeast, take I-93 North to I-293 North. Exit left to NH 101 (Bedford-Goffstown); at junction of NH 101 and NH 114 (set of lights), take NH 114 North. Continue through a set of lights (Mini Golf and restaurant on right) to St. Anselm Dr. (next set of lights). The abbey is in about 1 mile.

From points southwest, take US 3 North. Continue to Everett Turnpike North to NH 101. Then proceed as above.

From the New Hampshire Seacoast or points west, take NH 101 to NH 114 and continue as above.

Public Transportation: There is air and bus service to Manchester. Contact guest master for further information.

History: Monks from St. Mary's Abbey, New Jersey, established St. Anselm Abbey in 1889 with a twofold mission: to open a college and to minister to the local German-speaking population. The monastery was named in honor of an 11th-century abbot, Archbishop of Canterbury, and doctor of the church. Both monastery and college have grown to a community of 30 monks and 2,000 students. The college is coeducational. In January 2008 St. Anselm College received worldwide attention when it hosted a nationally televised U.S. presidential debate.

Description: The monastery and college are set on a 300-acre campus on a hilltop overlooking Manchester, New Hampshire's largest city.

Star Island

30 Middle St., Portsmouth, NH 03801

Order: Owned and operated by the Star Island Corporation (Unitarian Universalists and the United Church of Christ/Congregationalists)

Contact: Star Island Corporation

Telephone: 603-430-6272. **Best time to call:** Mon. to Fri., 9 AM to 5 PM

Web site: www.starisland.org; **e-mail:** personalretreats@starisland.org

Accommodations: Star Island offers a wide variety of accommodations for guests in the Oceanic House, the hotel annex, small cottages, and motel units.

Meals: Breakfast, lunch, and dinner are served family-style in the Oceanic Dining Room. Reservations are recommended (603-601-0832). There is also a snack bar. Both are in the Oceanic House.

Costs: Contact the Star Island Corporation for information regarding current charges for room and meals. MasterCard, Visa, and personal check are accepted.

Directions: Star Island is 10 miles southeast of Portsmouth, N.H. From Portsmouth the *Thomas Laighton* sails to Star Island. For reservations call 800-441-4620 or 603-431-5500. The *Uncle Oscar,* which departs from Rye, N.H., also sails to the island. Call 603-964-6446.

History: Star Island is one of nine islands known as the Isles of Shoals. Discovered by John Smith in 1614, they were named for the schools (or shoals) of fish in the surrounding waters. The Isles were an important center for commerce in colonial times. In the 19th century, grand hotels were built here. One of them, the Oceanic House, is the largest building on Star Island. Summer conferences have been held here since 1897, and in 1916 the Star Island Corporation was formed. Though the corporation is headed by Unitarian Universalists and Congregationalists, the island, its facilities, and its programs are open to all.

Description: Star Island may aptly be described as a place of rugged beauty. There has been a chapel on the island's highest point since 1685. The second chapel was built of timbers from a Spanish ship in 1720, and the present stone meetinghouse has stood here since 1800. They have served over the centuries variously as a place of worship, a courthouse, a town meeting hall, and a school. "Today, candlelight chapel services are a cherished Star Island tradition. At the close of each day, Shoalers gather at the foot of the hill and form a procession, carrying candle lanterns as the villagers of long ago carried their whale-oil lamps up the same winding path to the meeting house. Inside the chapel, the candle lanterns are hung on brackets from the walls, providing the only source of light."

Points of Interest: Portsmouth is New Hampshire's only seaport and at one time was its capital. Dating to 1623, the town is rich in colonial history. Visit Strawbery Banke, a restored colonial neighborhood with many historic houses, some of which are open to the public.

Special Note: "Amidst the natural beauty of an island environment, Star is a place for families, teens, and adults to experience religion, spirituality, and a feeling of community. It is a place to learn and grow, to form lifelong bonds of friendship, and to come back to the world with a renewed sense of hope and caring."

> *They that go down to the sea in ships,*
> *That do business in great waters;*
> *These see the works of the Lord,*
> *And his wonders in the deep.*
>
> —PSALM 107

✤ NEW JERSEY

Convent of St. John Baptist and St. Marguerite's House

P.O. Box 240, 82 West Main St., Mendham, NJ 07945

Order: Community of St. John Baptist (Episcopal)

Contact: Guest Mistress

Telephone: 973-543-4641. Best times to call: 10 AM to 12 noon and 1 PM to 5 PM

Web site: www.csjb.org; **e-mail:** csjb@csjb.org

Accommodations: Convent houses six female guests, and St. Marguerite's Retreat House accommodates 26 guests (men and women), each in a single room and all with shared baths.

Meals: Three meals daily

Costs: $65 per person per day for room and meals

Directions: From points north, take I-80 or I-78 to I-287 South. Exit at Morristown NJ 124 West. At Morristown Green, turn right on Washington St. (Route 24). Continue 8 miles to Mendham. The convent is on left.

From points south, take the Garden State Parkway or New Jersey Turnpike to I-287 North. Exit at 22B. Follow US 206 North to Chester. Turn right on Route 24 East and continue 5 miles to Mendham. The convent is on right.

Public Transportation: Contact the guest mistress.

History: The Community of St. John Baptist was begun in Windsor, England, in 1852 by Harriet Monsell, the widow of an Anglican priest, and the Reverend Thomas T. Carter. The purpose of the foundation was twofold: to engage in both contemplative prayer and active service. In 1874 the community came to the United States, first taking up residence in New York City and later moving to its rural and peaceful surroundings in New Jersey. St. Marguerite's Retreat House was built in 1908. At first a children's home, it became a retreat house in 1960.

Description: St. Marguerite's Retreat House is a redbrick re-creation of an English manor house. Beautiful trees and shrubs surround St. Marguerite's, and beyond is a 93-acre woodland "which lends itself to prayer and meditation. Walking paths provide guests with the opportunity to experience God's beauty in nature." Just across the way is the Gothic Revival, white-stuccoed convent. Guests are invited to join the sisters at their daily services in the chapel.

Point of Interest: Just 8 miles down the road is Morristown National Historical Park. This was the main encampment for George Washington and his men for two winters during the American Revolution.

St. Mary's Abbey
Delbarton

230 Mendham Rd., Morristown, NJ 07960

Order: Benedictine Monks (Roman Catholic)

Contact: Guest Master

Telephone: 201-538-3231. **Best time to call:** 8 AM to 5 PM

Web site: www.osbmonks.org; **e-mail:** osbmonks@delbarton.org

Accommodations: Abbey Retreat Center houses up to 66 guests, in 34 single and twin-bedded rooms, all with shared baths.

Meals: Three meals daily

Costs: $60 per person per day for room and meals

Directions: From New York City take the George Washington Bridge and follow I-95 to I-80 West. Exit at I-287 South and take I-287 to Morristown Exit 35 (NJ 124; old 24/Madison Ave.). Bear right at end of ramp onto NJ 124 West (South St.). Proceed straight 1 mile to the Morristown Green. Drive three sides of the green (do not take US 202). Follow the sign for 510 West (Washington St.). This becomes Route 24 (Mendham Rd.). St. Mary's will be on left—2.5 miles from Morristown Green. Alternately, from New York City via the Lincoln Tunnel, take Route 3 West to US 46 West to I-80 West. Then proceed as above.

From points east or west, take I-80. From points north or south take I-287. Take the Morristown exit 35 and proceed as above.

Public Transportation: Contact guest master for information.

History: St. Mary's was founded in Newark, New Jersey, in 1857. The Morristown property—a former country estate—was bought in 1926. Thirty years later—in 1956—the abbot and monks made the move to Morristown. True to Benedictine tradition, the monks teach at Delbarton (a prep school for boys), offer hospitality to retreatants, and minister to parishes here and in Brazil.

Description: Delbarton is the name of the former estate that the abbey occupies today. The large granite mansion has a lovely Italian garden, complete with classical statuary. Farther up the hill is the abbey church, its red brick and starkly modern exterior contrasting sharply with the "Old Main" estate house. The abbey has 360 wooded acres with paths and splendid views of the countryside beyond.

Point of Interest: During the Revolutionary War, George Washington and the soldiers of the Continental Army camped for two winters in what is now Morristown National Historical Park.

❖ NEW MEXICO

Monastery of Christ in the Desert

P.O. Box 270, Forest Service Rd. 151, Abiquiu, NM 87510

Order: Benedictine Monks (Roman Catholic)

Contact: Guest Master

Telephone: 801-5345-8567

Web site: www.christdesert.org; **e-mail:** cidguestmaster@christdesert .org

Accommodations: Guest house accommodates up to 17 individuals in nine single and four double rooms, all with shared baths.

Meals: Three meals daily

Costs: There is no fixed charge, but $60 per person per day would cover the monastery's cost.

Directions: The monastery is about 75 miles north of Santa Fe and about 53 miles south of Chama, New Mexico, off US 84. About 1 mile south of the entrance sign for Echo Amphitheater, or 1 mile north of the Ghost Ranch Piedra Lumbre Education and Visitor Center of the Carson National Forest (not to be confused with the Ghost Ranch itself), the road for the monastery leaves US 84 toward the west. (If coming from Santa Fe to the north, turn left). Forest Service Road 151 (the road to the monastery) is 13 miles long, winding, steep, and narrow at some points. It has a dirt and clay surface and becomes very slippery when wet.

Public Transportation: There is no public transportation to monastery.

History: Three monks from Mount Saviour Monastery, New York, founded the Monastery of Christ in the Desert in 1964. The present monastic community began arriving in 1974 and is an abbey of the Subiaco Congregation of Benedictines.

Description: The church, convento, and guest house, built of stone and adobe, are in a canyon 6,500 feet above sea level. This is surrounded by wilderness. The nearest neighbor is about 15 miles away.

Points of Interest: Carson National Forest and Santa Fe National Forest are on either side of the monastery.

Special Note: It is essential to contact the guest master in advance for information on travel conditions, climate, and advice on what to bring.

> *Let all guests that come be received like Christ Himself, for He will say: "I was a stranger and ye took Me in."*
>
> —RULE OF SAINT BENEDICT

Our Lady of Guadalupe Benedictine Abbey
P.O. Box 1080, Pecos, NM 87552-1080

Order: Benedictine Monks and Oblate Sisters in two communities (Roman Catholic)

Contact: Reservation Office

Telephone: 505-757-6415 or 505-757-6600, ext. 266. Call Mon. to Fri. 9 AM to 11:30 AM or 1 PM to 3 PM, and Sat. 9 AM to 11:30 AM Mountain Time.

Web site: www.pecosmonastery.org; **e-mail:** guestmaster@pecosmona stery.org

Accommodations: Motel-style retreat units accommodate up to 60 guests in single and twin rooms, each with private bath.

Meals: Three meals daily

Costs: Contact Reservation Office for information regarding charges.

Directions: From Santa Fe, take I-25 North to Exit 299 (Pecos/Glorieta). Than take NM 50 for 7 miles into village of Pecos. Turn left (north) at stop sign onto NM 63. The abbey is on left in 0.5 mile, beyond bridge over Pecos River at northern end of village.

From the north on I-25, take Exit 307 (Rowe/Pecos). This exit leads directly to NM 63 North, and the village of Pecos is 5 miles down the highway. Proceed straight through the village to bridge over Pecos River. Abbey is on left 0.5 mile beyond bridge.

Public Transportation: There is direct air service to Santa Fe from Denver or Dallas. The alternative is to fly to Albuquerque. The abbey will advise on local bus service and pick up form either airport. In addition, Amtrak has service (on the Chicago–Los Angeles South-West Chief line) to nearby Lamy. Arrange in advance with the abbey for pickup on arrival.

History: The monastery began in 1955, when the property was purchased by the Benedictines of Benet Lake, Wisconsin. In 1964 four of the monks came to Pecos with the vision of establishing a charismatic Benedictine community. "As the community has developed, it has sought to deepen its monastic dimension; and although visible charismatic gifts are still to be enjoyed and shared, there is also a growing attention to the contemplative monastic tradition." In 1985 the community was joined to the Olivetan Congregation of the Benedictine Order.

Description: The 1,000-acre property is in the Sangre de Cristo ("Blood of Christ") Mountains at an altitude of 7,000 feet above sea level, located in the secluded Pecos River Valley.

Points of Interest: Santa Fe is 25 miles from the monastery. Guests may visit the many Native American reservations in the area.

Special Note: In addition to receiving individual guests, the abbey also offers group retreats. A $50 nonrefundable deposit is necessary to secure a reservation. Contact the Reservation Office for more information.

✤ NEW YORK

Abbey of the Genesee
3258 River Rd., Box 900, Piffard, NY 14533-0900

Order: Cistercian (Trappist) Monks (Roman Catholic)

Contact: Guest Master

Telephone: 716-243-2220

Web site: www.abbeyretreats.org or www.geneseeabbey.org; **e-mail:** guestrsv@frontiernet.net

Accommodations: Bethlehem House accommodates 15 guests in single rooms, all with shared baths. In addition, there are accommodations for up to 20 guests in Bethany House, and 12 in Nazareth House in rooms with two to four beds, all with shared baths.

Meals: Three meals daily in Bethlehem House. Guests may use the kitchen in Bethany and Nazareth houses to prepare their own meals.

Costs: Suggested donation of $50 per person per night

Directions: The Genesee Expressway (I-390) provides easy access by car to Geneseo. Traveling north or south along I-390, take Exit 8 for Geneseo and proceed west on US 20A through Geneseo. Turn right onto NY 63 North. In Piffard, turn right (at abbey sign) onto River Rd. (north).

From the west on the New York State Thruway (I-90), exit at Interchange 46, proceeding south on I-390 to Exit 8, as above.

From the east on the New York State Thruway (I-90), exit at Batavia and take NY 98 South to NY 63 South. In Piffard, turn left onto River Rd. North.

Public Transportation: The nearest airport is Greater Rochester International. There is also Amtrak service to Rochester, as well as Greyhound and Trailways bus service to Rochester. From Rochester, New York Trailways has bus service to Geneseo. Transportation may be arranged from the airport, bus station, or train station to the abbey for $50. The abbey can provide transportation from Geneseo if prior arrangement is made.

History: Trappist monks from Gethsemani Abbey in Kentucky arrived in the Genesee Valley in 1951, having accepted the gift of a tract of land. The community originally lived in what is now Bethlehem House. The abbey church was completed in 1975.

Description: The church is built of stone and designed to express "an appropriate blend of modern and traditional elements." Bethlehem House is 0.5 mile north of the church and abbey. Bethany House is a stately 19th-century cobblestone manse, while Nazareth House is a cedar dwelling.

Point of Interest: Letchworth State Park is a 15-minute drive south of the abbey.

Graymoor
Spiritual Life Center

P.O. Box 300, 1350 Route 9, Garrison, NY 10524

Order: Graymoor Friars (Roman Catholic)

Contact: Director

Telephone: 845-424-2111. **Best time to call:** Mon. to Fri. 9 AM to 5 PM Eastern Time

Web site: www.graymoorcenter.org; **e-mail:** graymoorcenter@atone mentfriars.org

Accommodations: St. Pius X Building/Graymoor Spiritual Life Center houses up to 110 guests in 55 double-occupancy rooms, and 25 guests in single rooms in the Old Friary (St. Paul's). There are two suites with private baths; the other rooms have shared baths.

Meals: Three meals daily

Costs: $65 per person per day for room and meals. For a weekend (Fri. to Sun.) it is $165 per person, single occupancy, or $115 per person, double occupancy.

Directions: Graymoor is on US 9, 4 miles north of Peekskill, New York, and 13 miles south of I-84, Exit 13.

Public Transportation: From Manhattan take the MTA Metro-North Hudson River Line from Grand Central Station to Peekskill. From Peekskill there is cab service to Graymoor.

History: Though a Roman Catholic order, the Franciscan Friars of the Atonement (or the Graymoor Friars, as they are popularly known) have their roots in the Episcopal Church. They and the Graymoor Sisters were founded by an Episcopal priest and a nun in 1898 and entered the Roman Catholic Church in 1909. The worldwide annual Week of Prayer for Christian Unity began here in 1908.

Description: Graymoor covers a wide expanse on a hill, and has several chapels, shrines, gardens, houses, and shops. Perhaps the most notable building is St. John the Baptist Church. Once an Episcopal chapel,

Graymoor gets its name from the church's rector (Gray) and a benefactor (Moore). A recent addition to Graymoor is the World Trade Center Cross. Placed here in 2002 by the Ironworkers of Local 40, it is made with materials salvaged from Ground Zero and is a memorial to those who perished on September 11, 2001.

Points of Interest: The Appalachian Trail passes through Graymoor. West Point, Stonecrop Gardens, and the Chuang Yen Buddhist Monastery are nearby.

Special Note: Graymoor sponsors a year-round calendar of retreats and special events. A brochure is available from the director.

Holy Cross Monastery

P.O. Box 99, West Park, NY 12493
1615 US 9W, Highland, NY 12528

Order: Order of the Holy Cross (Episcopal)

Contact: Guest Master

Telephone: 914-384-6660, ext. 3003

Web site: www.holycrossmonastery.com; **e-mail:** guesthouse@hcmnet .org

Accommodations: Guest house accommodates up to 39 persons, each in a single room and all with shared baths.

Meals: Three meals daily

Costs: $70 per weekday and $80 per weekend day is requested to cover the cost of room and meals.

Directions: Take the New York State Thruway (I-87) to Exit 18 (New Paltz), then take NY 299 East to US 9W. Go north 4 miles; monastery entrance will be on right.

Public Transportation: Take the MTA Metro-North train from Grand Central Station in Manhattan to Poughkeepsie. Contact guest master for further information.

History: The Order of the Holy Cross has the distinction of being the oldest indigenous men's community in the Episcopal Church. The Reverend James Otis Sargent Huntington founded the order in New York City in 1884, and he settled the order's motherhouse at West Park in 1904.

Description: The monastery sits on the banks of the Hudson River in the Mid-Hudson Valley. The guest house is the original monastery and is connected with the church and the newer monastery. Guests are welcome to join the community in worship and to dine with the monks in their refectory.

Points of Interest: West Park is situated directly across the Hudson River from Hyde Park, where one may visit the Vanderbilt Mansion National Historic Site as well as the Home of Franklin D. Roosevelt National Historic Site and the Roosevelt Presidential Library and Museum. West Point, historic Newburgh, which served as George Washington's headquarters during the last years of the Revolutionary War, and the Huguenot Street Historic District in New Paltz are also nearby.

House of the Redeemer

7 E. 95th St., New York, NY 10128

Order: Episcopal

Contact: Executive Director

Telephone: 212-289-0399

Web site: www.houseoftheredeemer.org; **e-mail:** info@redeem.org

Accommodations: Houses 18 guests in single and twin rooms, some with private baths.

Meals: Meals are provided for those participating in a group retreat of 12 or more. A kitchenette is available to individual guests at an additional cost.

Costs: $90 for a single and $115 for a twin-bedded room, each with a shared bath. $140 for a twin-bedded room with a private bath. There are reduced rates for clergy and members of religious orders, or for those participating in a group retreat.

Directions: From midtown Manhattan, head north on Madison Ave. and then left (west) on E. 95th St.

Public Transportation: Take a New York City Transit Madison Ave. bus (M1, M2, M3, or M4) to 95th St. By subway, take the 6 Line (Lexington Ave.) to 96th St.

History: The House of the Redeemer is the former Fabbri Mansion. Built between 1914 and 1916, it was the home of Edith Shepard (great-grand-daughter of Commodore Cornelius Vanderbilt) and her husband, Ernesto Fabbri. In 1949 Mrs. Fabbri converted her home into a retreat house, thereafter called the House of the Redeemer. It was designated a landmark by New York City's Landmarks Preservation Commission in 1974. Staffed by the Episcopal Community of St. Mary until 1982, the house is now under the stewardship of an independent board of trustees.

Description: Designed by architect Grosvenor Atterbury, the house was built in the style of an Italian Renaissance palazzo, or town house. The interior contains many exceptionally fine features, including the library, with woodwork from the 15th-century Ducal Palace in Urbino, Italy. Antiques, paintings, and original furnishings all contribute to the House of the Redeemer's status as a New York City landmark.

Special Note: The House of the Redeemer welcomes clergy visiting New York City on official business, as well as individuals who wish to retreat. The house offers many interesting programs throughout the year. There are services in the chapel Monday through Friday.

Little Portion Friary

P.O. Box 99, 48 Old Post Rd., Mt. Sinai, NY 11766

Order: Franciscan Brothers (Episcopal)

Contact: Secretary

Telephone: 631-473-0553. **Best time to call:** 9:30 AM to 1 PM Eastern Time

Web site: www.littleportionfriary.net; **e-mail:** contact@littleportion friary.net

Accommodations: Wayside House accommodates up to 16 guests in 10 single and three double rooms, all with shared baths.

Meals: Three meals daily

Costs: $85 per person per day for room and meals. Group rates are available.

Directions: The friary is in the geographic center of Long Island, near the intersection of Routes 25A, 347, and 83.

From New England there is ferry service from Bridgeport on the Bridgeport & Port Jefferson Steamboat Company.

Public Transportation: Take the Long Island Rail Road from Penn Station in Manhattan to Port Jefferson. Contact secretary for further information.

History: This community of Episcopal Franciscans was founded in Wisconsin in 1919 by the Reverend Joseph Cookston. Saint Francis and his brethren had a chapel at Portiuncula in 13th-century Italy, and in 1928 this, an American "Little Portion," was established on Long Island.

Description: The friary is on more than 60 acres bordering Mt. Sinai Harbor and its wildlife sanctuary. The area has been designated a historic district, and buildings at Little Portion reflect the simple lifestyle of the brothers.

Mount Saviour Monastery

231 Monastery Rd., Pine City, NY 14871-9787

Order: Benedictine Monks (Roman Catholic)

Contact: Guest Brother

Telephone: 607-743-1688

Web site: www.msaviour.org; **e-mail:** guest@msaviour.org

Accommodations: St. Joseph's Guest House accommodates 15 men in single rooms, all with shared baths. In addition, there are accommodations for seven women in three single and two twin-bedded rooms in St. Gertrude's Guest House. Married couples may also stay at St. Gertrude's or in the more private facilities of St. Peter's farmhouse, West Casa, and East Casa. Contact the guest brother for more detailed information.

Meals: Three meals daily. Men take meals with the monks in the monastery; women in St. Gertrude's. Private kitchens are available to those staying at St. Peter's farmhouse, East Casa, and West Casa.

Costs: Suggested offering of $55 per person per night. "We are grateful to those who can give more and welcome those whose means allow for less. The generosity of our guests permits us to run the guest houses and we are grateful for their support."

Directions: I-86 is the main highway from both east and west. From the east, take the Elmira exit, marked "Church Street Route 352." Follow Church St. through the city to NY 225. Turn left and continue 4 miles to Monastery Rd., on right.

From points west, take I-86 East to Exit 45. Proceed on NY 352 through Corning. At last traffic light, turn right on NY 225. (Be prepared to bear left just after you enter onto this road.) There are two turns, but they are well marked. Continue on 225 until you come to Monastery Rd. on left.

From points north or south, NY 14 crosses Church St. (NY 352) in Elmira. Head west on Church St. though town to NY 225; turn left, and continue to Monastery Rd. on right.

Public Transportation: There is air service to the Elmira/Corning Regional Airport (about 10 miles away). Taxi service is available. Bus service is also available to Elmira. If you are arriving before 5 PM, you may make arrangements with the guest brother to be met at the bus depot. If you arrive after 5 PM, please take a cab to the monastery.

History: Mount Saviour, named in honor of the Savior's Transfiguration, was established in 1951 by Father Damasus Winzen and three companions.

Description: Atop Mount Saviour are the monastery's octagonal chapel and towering spire. A 14th-century statue of the Virgin stands in the center of the chapel's crypt. Beyond the cluster of the chapel and monastery are more than 200 acres of woodlands and fields.

Points of Interest: The monastery is in the beautiful and fabled Finger Lakes region of New York State. Cornell University, the Corning Museum of Glass, and Quarry Farm (sometime home of Samuel Clemens) are nearby.

Special Note: Mount Saviour does not accommodate overnight-only guests. The minimum stay is two days, with most guests staying two to seven days. Group retreats may be held on special request. Further information may be obtained from the guest brother or online at the monastery's Web site.

New Skete Monastery
P.O. Box 128, New Skete Rd., Cambridge, NY 12816

Order: Monks, Companions, and Nuns (Orthodox Church in America)

Contact: Guest Master

Telephone: 518-677-3928. **Best time to call:** Tues. to Sat. 10 AM to 4 PM Eastern Time. The office is closed on Mon.

Web site: www.newsketemonks.com; **e-mail:** monks@newskete.com

Accommodations: Guest house accommodates up to five guests in three twin-bedded rooms.

Meals: Three meals daily, except Sun. and feast days, when breakfast is not served.

Costs: Suggested donation of $50 per person per day for room and meals

Directions: It is a three-and-a-half- to four-hour drive from Manhattan to New Skete. From Manhattan's West Side, take the Henry Hudson Parkway to the Saw Mill River Parkway. Continue on the Saw Mill River

Parkway to the Taconic Parkway (north) to NY 295 East. At NY 22, go north all the way to the town of Cambridge. In Cambridge, turn right at the stoplight onto Main St. and go 3 miles out of town to Chestnut Hill Rd.; turn right. Proceed on Chestnut Hill for 1 mile to New Skete Rd., which only goes left. Take the road to the monastery at the top of the hill.

From Manhattan's East Side take the FDR (East River Dr.) north and look for the Triborough Bridge. Take the Bruckner Expressway (I-278 north or east) and then watch for signs for the Hutchinson River Parkway. Take the parkway to I-684 North, which turns into NY 22 North. Stay on NY 22 all the way to Cambridge and then follow the directions above.

From Boston (a four-hour drive), take the Massachusetts Turnpike (I-90) West to NY 22 (Exit 83—the first exit in New York State). Go north on NY 22 all the way to the town of Cambridge, and then follow directions as above.

From Albany (a one-and-a-quarter-hour drive), take NY 7 East and then US 22 North to Cambridge, as above.

Public Transportation: At Albany International Airport, there is car rental. There is also train service from Albany to Saratoga Springs. Make arrangements in advance with the guest master to be met on arrival. Yankee Trails offers bus service to Bennington, Vermont, on weekdays only. The bus makes a stop in Hoosick Falls, New York. This is the closest bus stop to the monastery. Again, make advance arrangements with the guest master to be met on arrival.

History: By definition, a "skete" is a group of monks gathered around an elder. New Skete began in 1966 with a group of 12 monks under the leadership of Father Lawrence. They had been Roman Catholic Byzantine-rite Franciscans and received canonical permission to establish a new community living the principles of Eastern Christian monasticism. Since that time New Skete has grown to three separate communities: the Monks, the Nuns, and the Companions. The community was received into the Orthodox Church in 1978.

Description: The skete has about 500 acres of mountainous woodland at the far edge of the Taconic range. There are two churches, one built in the fashion of a traditional Russian wood church, and the other a more contemporary design with a spacious and elegant interior.

Points of Interest: There are two colonial battlefields in the area: Saratoga, New York, and Bennington, Vermont. Bennington is also the home of the Bennington Museum, which includes the Grandma Moses Schoolhouse Museum. Southeast of Cambridge is Williamstown, Massachusetts. There, visitors may visit the Sterling and Francine Clark Art Institute with its outstanding collection of European and American paintings, sculpture, and decorative arts.

Special Note: The monks are known far and wide for their breeding of German shepherds. They have authored *How to Be Your Dog's Best Friend* and other books about dog training.

Our Lady of the Resurrection Monastery
St. Scholastica Guest House
246 Barmore Rd., LaGrangeville, NY 12540

Order: Benedictine Monks (Roman Catholic)

Contact: Brother Victor-Antoine d'Avila-Latourrette

Web site: www.ourladyoftheresurrectionmonastery.webs.com

Accommodations: Guest house accommodates six guests in two single rooms and two twin-bedded rooms, all with shared baths.

Meals: The main meal of the day is served in the monastery; breakfast and lunch are self-prepared by guests in guest house.

Costs: Suggested donation of $70 per person per day

Directions: From the Taconic Parkway take Exit 55 (east). Take NY 82 1 mile north to Barmore Rd. and then turn right on Barmore to the monastery, which will be on right.

Public Transportation: There is train service from Grand Central Terminal in New York City to Poughkeepsie. It is then a 15-mile taxi ride to the monastery.

Description: In a secluded rural setting, the monastery and guest house are beautiful in their rustic simplicity. The chapel has Byzantine elements, and is a reflection of the monks' desire to work and pray for the unity of the churches of the East and West. There is a library, which guests may use. The Saint Joseph Workshop sells Monastery Artisanal Vinegars made by the monks as well as their dried herbs, herbal teas, pesto sauce, chutney, jams, tomato sauce, and relish. In addition, the Atelier Saint-Joseph, as the shop is also called, sells books, crèches, icons, note cards, and other items.

Points of Interest: LaGrangeville is in picturesque Dutchess County. Route 9D is a scenic road that runs parallel to the Hudson River, linking many charming towns and historic sites in the Hudson River Valley.

Special Note: The monastery's Brother Victor-Antoine D'Avila-Latourrette has authored several cookbooks, most recently, *The Pure Joy of Monastery Cooking.*

> *Idleness is an enemy to the soul; and hence at certain seasons the brethren ought to occupy themselves in the labour of their hands, and at others in holy reading.*
>
> —RULE OF SAINT BENEDICT

St. Margaret's House and Ecumenical Center
47 Jordan Rd, New Hartford, NY 13413-2385

Order: Ecumenical

Contact: Stewards

Telephone: 315-724-2324

Web site: www.smhec47.org; **e-mail:** smhec47@aol.com

Accommodations: St. Margaret's accommodates up to 24 guests in 16 single and four double rooms, each with its own sink and all with shared baths.

Meals: Three meals daily

Costs: Contact one of the stewards for current rates.

Directions: From the New York State Thruway (I-90), take Exit 31 and follow the signs to Genesee St. Turn right on Genesee St. and drive for 7 miles. After the New Hartford Shopping Center, turn left on Jordan Rd.

Public Transportation: There is air, train, and bus service to Utica. Contact the stewards for further information.

History: For many years St. Margaret's House belonged to the Society of St. Margaret, a community of sisters in the Episcopal Church.

Description: St. Margaret's, a stone Tudor Revival building, has 8 acres just south of Utica. The house is surrounded by lawns, trees, and gardens.

Special Note: In addition to opportunities for private retreats, group retreats are also offered here. Contact the stewards for information.

St. Mary's Convent
Christ the King Spiritual Life Center
575 Burton Rd., Greenwich, NY 12834

Order: Community of St. Mary (Anglican)

Contact: Mother Miriam, C.S.M.

Telephone: 518-692-3028 or 518-692-9550. **Best time to call:** 10 AM to noon, and 1 PM to 5 PM Eastern Time

Web site: www.stmaryseast.org or www.ctkcenter.org; **e-mail:** Mother Miriam@stmaryseast.org

Accommodations: Convent accommodates seven guests in three double rooms and one single-occupancy handicap-accessible room, each with a private bath. Christ the King Spiritual Life Center offers a variety of lodging options for individuals and groups.

Meals: Three meals daily

Costs: Current rates available on request

Directions: From points north or south take US 22, which is east of and parallel to the Hudson River. At Cambridge, New York, take NY 372 North to Greenwich.

From Massachusetts, take the Massachusetts Turnpike (I-90) west to US 22 North, then proceed as above.

Public Transportation: Contact convent for information.

History: The first religious community in the Episcopal Church, the order was founded by five women in New York City in 1865. In 1873 St. Mary's Convent was moved to Peekskill and, in 2004, moved to Greenwich. Here the sisters lead a traditional monastic life, staff Christ the King Spiritual Life Center, and work on their micro-farm, "using hand-tilled sustainable agriculture techniques."

Description: Newly built, the convent is a rambling building surrounded by woods and fields. Many statues and other objects from the sisters' previous convent embellish the chapel.

The Leo House

332 W. 23rd St., New York, NY 10011-2289

Order: Sisters of Saint Agnes (Roman Catholic)

Contact: Reservation Desk

Telephone: 800-732-2438 or 212-929-1010, ext. 219

Accommodations: House accommodates up to 100 guests in 70 rooms. Rooms are single, twin-bedded, or double-bedded. There is also a family room that accommodates up to six. Some rooms have full bath; others have a sink and toilet with shared showers.

Meals: An à la carte or full breakfast is served Mon. through Sat. Baking is done on premises. For other meals, the surrounding neighborhoods offer a wide variety of reasonably priced restaurants.

Costs: Rates per night for rooms with a single bed are $100 with a shower or $90 without a shower. Double-bedded rooms are $120 with a shower or $110 without a shower. Twin-bedded rooms are $125 with a shower or $115 without a shower. The family room has a shower and costs $190 per night. The cost of breakfast is $9 per person. Visa and MasterCard are accepted.

Directions: Keep in mind that 23rd St. is a two-way street running east and west across Manhattan. The Leo House is located on 23rd St. between Eighth and Ninth Aves.

Public Transportation: There are trains to Grand Central Station and Penn Station, and buses to Port Authority Bus Terminal. From each of these stations it is a short taxi ride to the Leo House. Alternately, take MTA M10 bus (Seventh/Eighth Aves.) southbound to 23rd St. By subway, take the Eighth Ave. line (red number 1, 2, or 3) to the 23rd St. Station. It is a half-block walk from the subway exit to The Leo House.

From JFK Airport, there are several options: One is Super Shuttle limousine service. Another is the New York Airport Service bus to Penn Station, Grand Central Station, or Port Authority Bus Terminal. There is also AirTrain, part of the MTA subway system.

From La Guardia, New York Airport Service provides bus service to Manhattan, and the Express Shuttle to midtown terminals.

From Newark Airport, Newark Liberty Airport Express Bus goes to the midtown terminals. AirTrain Newark connects the Newark monorail system to the New Jersey transit line to Penn Station.

History: The Leo House, founded in 1889, is named in honor of Pope Leo XIII. A Roman Catholic nonprofit organization, the house was begun by the St. Raphael Society to help newly arrived German immigrants. Leo-Haus, as it was first known, moved from the Battery Park neighborhood to its present site in 1926. Though the waves of German immigrants have subsided, the hospitality offered here has not.

Description: The Leo House is an eight-story building with Old World charm, complete with a comfortable and newly decorated lobby, a dining room, and a chapel. A peaceful garden is in the rear of the building, an ideal spot for reading, relaxing, and meditation. Within the noise and rush of the city, the Leo House is a haven for those seeking rest and reflection in their travels.

Points of Interest: The Leo House is in Chelsea, one of the liveliest and safest neighborhoods in New York. It is within walking distance of the Hudson River, Broadway theaters, Madison Square Garden, and many other midtown attractions.

Special Note: "The Leo House is a Catholic, non-profit guest house, dedicated to offering low cost, temporary hospitality to clergy and religious, persons visiting the sick, students, and travelers . . . People of all faiths are welcome."

> *Go into the city, and it shall be told thee what thou must do.*
>
> —ACTS 9:6

Transfiguration Monastery

701 New York Route 79, Windsor, NY 13865

Order: Camaldolese Benedictine Nuns (Roman Catholic)

Contact: Sister Donald Corcoran, Er. Cam.

Telephone: 607-655-2366

Web site: www.transfigurationmonastery.org

Accommodations: Guest house accommodates seven persons, in three single rooms, one twin-bedded room, and one sitting room/bedroom, all with shared bath.

Meals: Three meals daily

Costs: $35 to $40 per person per day

Directions: Take NY 17 to Exit 79 (Windsor), then NY 79 South for 3.5 miles. The monastery is on right, just before golf course.

Public Transportation: There is bus service to Binghampton, New York. Contact Sister Donald for further information.

History: Three Benedictine nuns were accepted into the Roman Catholic Diocese of Syracuse in 1975 to establish a Benedictine monastery. In 1979 they acquired a suitable property in New York's Southern Tier, where they built their simple and attractive monastery. In 1988 the community affiliated with the Camaldolese—a congregation of the Benedictine order. Begun by Saint Romuald in the 11th century at Camaldoli, Italy, these monasteries provide for the monastic lifestyle lived both in community and in hermitages.

Description: Transfiguration Monastery is set on 100 acres of woodland and arable river plain nestled at the foot of Horeb Mountain (the "Mountain of God"). Reflecting the nuns' simplicity of spirit and concern for ecology, the monastery is built with natural materials such as wood and stone. Passive solar energy and wood-burning stoves are used.

✤ NORTH DAKOTA

Assumption Abbey

P.O. Box A, Richardton, ND 58652

Order: Benedictine Monks (Roman Catholic)

Contact: Guest Master

Telephone: 701-974-3315. Best times to call: 8 AM to 11:30 AM and 12:30 PM to 4:30 PM Mountain Time

Web site: www.assumptionabbey.com

Accommodations: Abbey houses 100 guests in single rooms, seven of which have private baths.

Meals: Three meals daily

Costs: "Freewill offerings are gratefully accepted."

Directions: From Bismarck, take I-94 West; Richardton is 75 miles from Bismarck.

Public Transportation: There is Greyhound bus service to Richardton. Contact the guest master for further information.

History: Assumption Abbey has its roots in Switzerland. In 1888 monks from Einsiedeln Abbey came to the Dakota Territory, settling at Devil's Lake. The following year they moved to Richardton to minister to the German immigrants in southwestern North Dakota. By 1911 the abbey church, the monastic quadrangle, and other buildings serving the community were completed. Today Assumption Abbey is home base to 65 monks, 30 of whom minister to Native Americans and others in North Dakota, as well as in several other states and in South America.

Description: The massive abbey church was designed in the Bavarian Romanesque style, its interior delineated by lofty arches. Fifty-two stained-glass windows light the church, its nave guarded by 24 saints depicted on canvas. Beyond the church there are a pottery, a print shop and book bindery, a communications center, a woodcraft shop, an apiary, and a 2,000-acre ranch with 300 head of cattle. Guests are welcome to walk the surrounding open fields, woods, and the serene shores of Abbey Lake.

> *The monastery, however, ought if possible to be so constituted that all things necessary, such as water, a mill, and a garden, and the various crafts may be contained within it . . .*
>
> —RULE OF SAINT BENEDICT

✤ OHIO

St. Andrew Svorad Abbey

10510 Buckeye Rd., Cleveland, OH 44104-3725

Order: Benedictine Monks (Roman Catholic)

Contact: Guest Master

Telephone: 216-721-5300. Best times to call: Mon. to Fri. 8:30 AM to 7:30 PM, and Sat. and Sun. 9 AM to 7 PM Eastern Time

Web site: www.bocohio.org; **e-mail:** brmario@juno.com

Accommodations: Guest-quarters wing of monastery houses up to 10 persons in single twin-bedded rooms, all with private baths.

Meals: Three meals daily

Costs: Freewill offering

Directions: From points east or west on I-80 (Ohio Turnpike), take interchange to I-480 northbound. This will merge with I-271. Exit I-271 at Chagrin Blvd. Go left off ramp to Richmond Rd. Continue to Shaker Blvd., turning left (Shaker Blvd. has a wide median dividing east- and westbound traffic. Cross eastbound Shaker Blvd. in order to turn left onto Shaker Blvd. westbound). Continue westbound on Shaker Blvd. for approximately 5.5 to 6 miles to Martin Luther King Jr. Dr. Turn left onto the drive (moving to the right lane). Just beyond second traffic light, on right, there is a church on corner, followed by Benedictine High School. The abbey drive is between the church and high school. Turn right onto the property. There is parking in front of abbey church.

From points east or west on I-90, take interchange to I-271 southbound. Exit I-271 at Chagrin Blvd. At bottom of exit ramp, turn right on Richmond Rd. Proceed to Shaker Blvd. and continue as above.

Driving east on I-90 toward downtown Cleveland, you will cross I-71. Continue east on I-90. It will become I-490, ending at East 55th St. Turn left onto East 55th (northbound) for 0.5 mile. Turn right onto Woodland Ave. (eastbound) for 1 mile. Turn right onto Buckeye Rd. (eastbound). Stay on Buckeye for 1 mile. Turn right onto Martin Luther King Jr. Dr. and follow directions above.

Driving north on I-71 or I-77 toward downtown Cleveland, take I-490 eastbound until it ends at East 55th St., and then continue as above.

Public Transportation: Take Rail Rapid Transit lines 67X (Blue Line: Van Aken) or 67AX (Green Line: Shaker). Alternately, take Bus Rapid Transit routes 10, 11, or 13 (Woodhill Rd.) or Route 50 (E. 116th St.).

History: The abbey was founded by and for members of Cleveland's Slovak-American community. In 1922 Slovak monks from the predominately Czech St. Procopius Abbey (Illinois) came to Cleveland to staff St. Andrew Parish. The budding Benedictine monastery became an independent priory in 1929 and was raised to the status of an abbey five years later. As the community and its works grew, so did its physical presence. Today St. Andrew Svorad Abbey has about 30 monks who live the Benedictine ideal of "work and prayer" at the abbey, the Benedictine High School, in parishes, and in various chaplaincies.

Description: The abbey is in the Buckeye-Woodland neighborhood of southeast Cleveland on 16 wooded acres at a high point overlooking the city.

Points of Interest: The neighborhood surrounding the abbey has a large Hungarian population. Of particular note is St. Elizabeth of Hungary Church, the oldest Hungarian Roman Catholic Church in America. About 1 mile north of St. Andrew's is the largest cluster of cultural institutions in the country, including Cleveland's Institute of Art, Institute of Music, Museum of Art and other museums, the Western Reserve Historical Society, and Severance Hall (home to the Cleveland Orchestra). Case Western Reserve University, the Cleveland Clinic and other hospitals, and notable churches of many denominations are also there.

Special Note: If planning an overnight visit to the abbey, a two-week prior notification is strongly suggested.

✤ OREGON

Mount Angel Abbey

1 Abbey Dr., St. Benedict, OR 97373

Order: Benedictine Monks (Roman Catholic)

Contact: Guest Master

Telephone: 503-845-3025. **Best time to call:** Mon. to Fri., 9 AM to 4 PM Pacific Time

Web site: www.mountangelabbey.org/retreat-house/index.html; **e-mail:** retreat@mtangel.edu

Accommodations: Retreat House accommodates up to 60 guests in 23 double-bedded and seven twin-bedded rooms, all with private baths. (Rooms may be single-occupancy.)

Meals: "Meals are an option for guests."

Costs: For single occupancy, $46 per person per day for room only, $77 for room and three meals. For double occupancy, $124 for two people per day for room and meals, or $63 for lodging only.

Directions: Mount Angel is about 40 miles south of Portland. From points north or south take I-5, then OR 214 12 miles to the village of Mount Angel. At the center of the village there is a fountain where there is a green directional sign for abbey.

Public Transportation: There is Amtrak service to Salem, and airport shuttle service to Woodburn. Visitors to Mount Angel can arrange for a pickup from either location. Contact guest master for information.

History: "Mount Angel" is the English translation of the German "Engelberg." When the abbey was founded by monks from the Swiss Abbey of Engelberg in 1882, it was built atop a hill that the Indians called "Tap-a-la-ma-ho," or Mountain of Communion with God, as they would contemplate the beauty of God's creation here. The monks established a day school, college, and seminary. From 1892 to 1966 their press published a weekly German-language newspaper and periodicals. The abbey was destroyed by fire twice (1892 and 1926), and all the buildings on site date from 1928 and later. The Retreat House was completed in 1959.

Description: The abbey overlooks the Willamette Valley and enjoys panoramic views—north, east, and south. Visitors are welcome to tour the abbey grounds and to visit the Abbey Museum and the Russian Center and Museum. Of particular note is the Mount Angel Abbey Library, designed in the 1960s by Finnish architect Alvar Aalto.

Priory of Our Lady of Consolation

23300 Walker Ln., Amity, OR 97101

Order: Brigittine Monks (Roman Catholic)

Contact: Guest Master

Telephone: 503-835-8080. **Best time to call:** 9 AM to 5 PM Pacific Time

Web site: www.brigittine.org; **e-mail:** monks@brigittine.org

Accommodations: Monastery houses up to 6 guests in single rooms, all with shared baths.

Meals: Thee meals daily

Costs: $35 per person per day for room and meals

Directions: From Portland take OR 99W southwest to Amity. In Amity turn onto Fifth Street. Keep left on Broadmead Rd., and then make a right onto Monastery Ln.

From points south take I-5 north to Salem, then OR 22 west to Rickreall, where you pick up OR 99W north to Amity.

Public Transportation: Contact the guest master for information.

History: The Order of the Most Holy Savior was founded by St. Birgitta of Sweden in 1370. In her honor, her monks and nuns are known as Brigittines. Here the monks support themselves through the making and selling of the Brigittine Monks Gourmet Confections. Twelve monks produce up to 1,500 pounds of candy a day. The have won the Medallion of Excellence from *Chocolate Magazine,* and critics have acclaimed their fudge to be the "world's finest." Guests may visit the Tasting Room at the monastery.

Description: The monastery and guest house are in the lush Willamette Valley. The guest house includes a library and parlor.

Trappist Abbey of Our Lady of Guadalupe
9200 NE Abbey Rd., Lafayette, OR 97127-0097

Order: Cistercian (Trappist) Monks (Roman Catholic)

Contact: Guest Master

Telephone: 503-852-0107. **Best time to call:** 9 AM to noon Pacific Time, weekdays.

Web site: www.trappistabbey.org; **e-mail:** community@trappistabbey .org

Accommodations: Four cottages, each with a shared bath at mid-level between floors, accommodate two guests—one upstairs and one downstairs.

Meals: Three meals daily

Costs: $50 per person per day

Directions: From Portland, take I-5 South to the Tigard/OR 99W exit. Turn right and stay on 99W for 26 miles to Lafayette. In Lafayette, drive to the west end. Turn off 99W onto Bridge St. (sign also says "Trappist Abbey") and go north 3 miles, staying on the surface road. The abbey is on right.

Public Transportation: Contact guest master for information.

History: The Cistercians began at the Abbey of Citeaux (near Dijon, France), where the monks wished to live the Rule of Saint Benedict in greater poverty, seclusion, and strictness. The work of Saint Bernard of Clairveaux in 1115 began an enormous expansion of the Cistercian Order throughout Europe. The name "Trappist" is derived from the Cistercian Abbey of La Trappe in Normandy, France. La Trappe was reformed in the late 17th century. In 1790, when all religious houses were suppressed because of the French Revolution, the community of La Trappe took refuge in Switzerland. In time the community returned to France and the congregation flourished again. Today there are about 100 Trappist monasteries of men and of women worldwide. Our Lady of Guadalupe Abbey began in 1948 at Pecos, New Mexico. As this was not an ideal place for the farming they wanted to pursue, the monks moved to Oregon in 1955. The abbey's patron, Our Lady of Guadalupe, "was chosen because of the Mexican influence in the Southwest, but gladly brought along to the Northwest." Today the abbey numbers nearly 30 monks, ranging in age from 30s to 90s.

Description: The abbey is built amid farm fields, tall firs, and other trees. The village of guest cottages, near the abbey church, is surrounded by grassy areas and ponds. There are paths leading to an 800-acre wooded hillside.

✤ PENNSYLVANIA

Community of Celebration

P.O. Box 309, 809 Franklin Ave., Aliquippa, PA 15001

Order: Community of Celebration (Episcopal)

Contact: Guest Mistress

Telephone: 724-375-1510. **Best time to call:** Mon. to Fri. 9 AM to 5 PM Eastern Time

Web site: www.communityofcelebration.com; **e-mail:** mail@community ofcelebration.com

Accommodations: Houses up to 12 guests in two guest houses and up to six guests in households.

Meals: Three meals daily

Costs: "General donations accepted"

Directions: Take I-80 and exit onto I-79 southbound. Follow I-79 to the Sewickley exit. Exit to right. At bottom of ramp, turn left at stop sign; this road will cross back under I-79. At next stop sign, turn right; ramp takes you onto PA 65. Follow 65 to Ambridge. (You will pass through business sections of Sewickley and Lansdale.) You will see Ambridge Bridge on left. At traffic light before bridge, turn right. Go about two blocks and turn left at next light. This is Maplewood Ave. in Ambridge. Follow Maplewood to next traffic light and turn left. The Ambridge Bridge will be in front of you. Cross bridge and turn right onto PA 51. Follow 51, getting off at first exit to right, Aliquippa. The ramp will come to a T. Turn left. Continue past two traffic lights. Just beyond third traffic light and on left side are the community's office and row houses.

Public Transportation: Pittsburgh International Airport is a 15-minute drive from Aliquippa. Guests can be met on arrival at airport with prior arrangement. There is also bus service from Pittsburgh. Contact guest mistress for further information.

History: The Society of the Community of Celebration was first established in England and Scotland. In 1965 the community's "extended family" Christian lifestyle was adopted by many in Houston, Texas. Formally established in 1972, in 1985 the group moved to Aliquippa, a once-thriving steel town, there to work and pray for the regeneration of the town's economy, environment, and social and spiritual health. Differing from traditional monastic orders, the community's membership includes men and women, married and single, adults and children, clergy and laity. They do, however, take traditional Benedictine vows and live simply on subsistence salaries and under the authority of the community's chapter.

Description: The community owns a series of three-story brick row houses and a separate house with a chapel, meeting room, and office space—all adjacent to the Chapel Garden. The row house properties have been developed to maximize green space. The backyards of twelve houses are combined to form one expansive lawn—an open, green refuge in an otherwise urban environment.

Points of Interest: Just across the Ohio River from Aliquippa is Ambridge, the site of Old Economy Village. The village was the home of the Harmonists, a 19th-century Christian communal society best known for its piety and industrial prosperity. Trinity Episcopal School for Ministry is also in Ambridge. Farther afield, a 40-minute drive to the southeast, is Pittsburgh, with its many cultural amenities, museums, planetarium, riverboat cruises, and professional and collegiate sporting events.

Special Note: The community sells worship resources (books, sheet music, CDs, DVDs, cards, and more) through its mail-order catalog.

Pendle Hill

338 Plush Mill Rd., Wallingford, PA 19086-6023

Order: Society of Friends/Quakers

Contact: Registrar

Telephone: 800-742-3150 or 610-566-4507. Best times to call: 9 AM to 12:30 PM and 1:30 to 5 PM Eastern Time

Web site: www.pendlehill.org; **e-mail:** registrar@pendlehill.org

Accommodations: Houses up to 35 guests in single and double rooms

Meals: Three meals daily

Costs: Contact registrar for current rates

Directions: From New Jersey and points north, take New Jersey Turnpike south to Exit 6, then I-276 (Pennsylvania Turnpike) west to Exit 25A. Take I-476 south to Chester; take Exit 2, turning right to Baltimore Pike. From Baltimore Pike take first left onto Turner Rd. (the median strip ends just at the intersection with Turner Rd.). Take second left onto Plush Mill Rd. Pendle Hill is about 200 yards on right.

From Philadelphia, take I-95 South to Exit 7, then I-476 North to Exit 2, then turn left onto Baltimore Pike. Continue as above.

From Washington, D.C., Baltimore, and Wilmington, take I-95 North to Exit 7, then I-476 North to Exit 2. Make left onto Baltimore Pike. Continue as above.

Public Transportation: From Philadelphia International Airport, there are three options for transportation to Pendle Hill: (1) Charles Barclay Airport Transfer Service (reserve in advance; call 800-697-9666); (2) SuperShuttle; or (3) taxi.

There is rail and bus service to Center City, Philadelphia. From there, take the SEPTA Media/Elwyn Local Train (R3) from Market St. East, Suburban Station, or 30th St. Station to Wallingford. For SEPTA fare and schedule information call 215-580-7800 or visit www.septa.com.

History: The Quakers (or Society of Friends) have their roots in England. In 1652, their founder, George Fox, visited Pendle Hill, in the northwest of England, where he was inspired by a vision. When the Quaker leader William Penn acquired vast lands west of the Delaware River, he named it Pennsylvania (or Penn's Wood) to honor his father. From that time to this day there has been a strong Quaker presence in this area. Pendle Hill was begun by Quakers in 1930 as a center for study and contemplation. It is open to all. Its educational philosophy is rooted in four basic social testimonies of Friends:

- Equality (of opportunity and respect for individuals)
- Simplicity (of the educational and material environment)
- Harmony (of inward and outward actions)
- Community (in daily life and in the seeking of the Spirit)

Description: Pendle Hill is a lovely 23-acre campus planted with about 100 species of trees and flowering shrubs. It has an organic garden, a spacious playground for children, and walking paths through wooded areas. Its 16 Georgian Revival buildings include living quarters, classrooms and meeting spaces, a bookstore, an art studio, and a library with 12,000 volumes, periodicals, and a special collection of Quaker books. Swarthmore College is within walking distance.

Points of Interest: Pendle Hill is in suburban Philadelphia, and guests may enjoy the city's historic sites, museums, and many other cultural amenities. Winterthur Museum is nearby in Delaware. It has an outstanding collection of American decorative arts spanning the years 1640–1840. Longwood Gardens is also in this, the Brandywine Valley. The former estate of the late Pierre S. du Pont, the gardens and expansive greenhouses are, without question, one of the most outstanding horticultural displays in America.

Special Note: Weekend conferences and retreats, four-day courses, and a resident study program are offered at Pendle Hill.

> *As we travelled, we came near a very great hill, called Pendle Hill [England], and I was moved of the Lord to go up to the top of it; which I did with difficulty, it was so very steep and high. When I was come to the top, I saw the sea bordering upon Lancashire. From the top of this hill the Lord let me see in what places he had a great people to be gathered.*
>
> —George Fox, 1652

St. Emma Monastery
Retreat House and Monastic Guest House

1001 Harvey Ave., Greensburg, PA 15601-1494

Order: Benedictine Nuns (Roman Catholic)

Contact: Mother Mary Anne Noll, O.S.B., Prioress

Telephone: 724-834-3060

Web site: www.stemma.org; **e-mail:** Benedictinenuns@stemma.org

Accommodations: Retreat House accommodates up to 52 guests, each in a single room with a sink, and all with shared baths. Each room has a ceiling fan, and the lounge, chapel, dining room, and conference rooms are air-conditioned. In addition, the Monastic Guest House has nine air-conditioned rooms with double beds, each with private bath. One room is handicapped accessible. The Monastic Guest House also has an oratory, laundry, and kitchen.

Meals: Thee meals daily

Costs: Contact monastery for current costs

Directions: The monastery is approximately 30 miles southeast of Pittsburgh. From the Pennsylvania Turnpike (I-76) traveling west, take Exit 57 to US 22 East. Make a right onto PA 819 (Harvey Rd.) South and drive 5 miles to monastery.

From the Pennsylvania Turnpike driving east, take Exit 75 and then US 119 North to PA 819 (Harvey Rd.) North to monastery.

Public Transportation: Contact monastery for information.

History: St. Emma's Monastery has its roots in the 900-year-old St. Walburg Abbey, Eichstaett, Bavaria. It was in 1931 that nine sisters from the abbey made the journey to Latrobe, Pennsylvania, to work and cook at St. Vincent's Archabbey. They later acquired their property in Greensburg, building the chapel in the 1950s and the monastery and re-treat house in 1960. It is interesting to note that in the early 1960s, St. Emma's helped pioneer the use of English in the daily office sung to tra-ditional Gregorian chant.

Description: The monastery has three chapels including the Walburga Shrine, which has a series of old German stained-glass windows. The chapels and other buildings are on the corner of a 100-acre farm with additional wooded acreage cushioning it from the surrounding area. There is an orchard, and the manicured grounds include outdoor Stations of the Cross, the Rosary Walk, and a life-size Crucifixion group overlooking the monastic cemetery.

Point of Interest: St. Vincent's Archabbey, founded by Bavarian monks in 1846, is 12 miles from St. Emma's.

Special Note: "We are a small Benedictine contemplative community of nuns whose life is centered around the Liturgy of the Hours and the daily celebration of the Eucharist. Guests are welcome to join us in our Cor Jesu Monastic Chapel for these times of prayer if they desire."

❖ RHODE ISLAND

Portsmouth Abbey

Cory's Lane, Portsmouth, RI 02871

Order: Benedictine Monks (Roman Catholic)

Contact: Guest Master

Telephone: 401-643-1285 or 401-683-2000.

Web site: www.portsmouthabbey.org; **e-mail:** brojoe@portsmouth abbey.org

Accommodations: Monastery accommodates up to seven male guests, in single rooms, one with private bath.

Meals: Three meals daily

Costs: "Guests who can are asked to make an offering—$20 to $25 a day is suggested."

Directions: From the greater Boston area, take Route 128 South to Route 24 South. Continue on Route 24 through Fall River and into Rhode Island, where Route 24 merges with, and becomes, Route 114 South. Continue south on 114 for a short distance. Make a right on Cory's Lane. Abbey is on right.

From New York City and Connecticut, take I-95 North. In Providence, Rhode Island, take I-195 East to Fall River, Massachusetts, then Route 24 South as above.

Public Transportation: There is air, train, and bus service to Providence, Rhode Island. From Kennedy Plaza in Providence take RIPTA bus #60 (marked "Newport"). Be sure bus takes W. Main Rd. route. Get off at Cory's Ln. and walk about 0.25 mile to abbey.

There is Peter Pan Bus service from Boston's South Station; ask driver to let you off at Portsmouth Town Hall. Contact guest master in advance to be met on arrival.

History: Leonard Sargent, a monk of Downside Abbey (England) and a former member of the Episcopal Order of the Holy Cross, founded this monastery of the English Benedictine Congregation in 1918. He was joined by other monks, Dom Hugh Diman among them. Dom Hugh had been an Episcopal deacon and the founder of St. George's School, Middletown, Rhode Island. In 1926 he opened a second prep school at Portsmouth Priory. The priory became an abbey in 1969.

Description: The abbey property, protected and surrounded by a cross-topped hill, placid Narragansett Bay, and a golf course, includes 500 acres of woods, farmland, fields, and landscaped campus. You'll see the old manor house. Built by Richard Upjohn as a summer cottage in the 1860s, it later became the first monastery. The newer monastery and church, designed by Pietro Belluschi, were completed in 1960. The church contains some notable works of art including a medieval stone statue of the Madonna, furniture made by Japanese American artist George Nakashima, and a large wire sculpture radiating from the altar crucifix. The sculpture is the work of Richard Lippold, whose art is also in the collection of New York's Metropolitan Museum of Art. A more recent addition to the abbey is the wind turbine, which may be seen for miles around.

Points of Interest: The Green Animals Topiary Garden is across the lane from the abbey, and Newport is 7 miles south on Route 114. There you may wish to continue your drive along the 10-mile Ocean Dr. or enjoy the fabled Cliff Walk. Newport abounds with sites of historic interest: The Quaker Meeting House (1699), Trinity Episcopal Church (1725), Touro Synagogue (1759), the Newport Mansions (www.newportmansions.org), and St. Mary's Church (1848), where John F. Kennedy and Jacqueline Bouvier were wed. The Church of S. John the Evangelist (Episcopal) in Newport hosts British choirs during its annual Celebration of English Cathedral Music.

❖ SOUTH CAROLINA

Mepkin Abbey

1098 Mepkin Abbey Rd., Moncks Corner, SC 29461

Order: Cistercian (Trappist) Monks (Roman Catholic)

Contact: Guest Master

Telephone: 803-761-8509. **Best time to call:** 8:30 AM to 4:30 PM Eastern Time

Web site: www.mepkinabbey.org; **e-mail:** guestmaster@mepkinabbey.org

Accommodations: Guest house welcomes up to 12 individuals, in single rooms, most with private bath. ("Married couples can be accommodated.")

Meals: Three meals daily

Costs: "Contributions are greatly appreciated."

Directions: From Charleston or I-95, take US 52 to the town of Moncks Corner. From town take Route 17A across the Tale Race Canal/Dennis Bishop Bridge. A short distance beyond the bridge (0.3 mile), turn right onto Route 402. Follow 402 for about 2 miles to the Rembert Dennis public boat landing/recreation. Note the Mepkin Abbey sign. Cross the tiny Wadboo Bridge and make an immediate right turn onto Dr. Evans Rd. Follow road for 6 miles; entrance to Mepkin Abbey will be on right. Drive down oak-lined lane to log Reception Center. Guest master will meet you when you ring the big bell.

Public Transportation: There is Greyhound, Amtrak, and air service to Charleston, and Greyhound offers bus service to Moncks Corner. Contact guest master in advance about being met on arrival.

History: *Mepkin* is an Indian word meaning "serene and lovely." From colonial times up until the early 20th century, 600 acres here were used as a rice farm. Henry Laurens (president of the Continental Congress) bought this land before the American Revolution, and he is buried here. In 1936 the plantation was bought by Henry R. Luce, publisher/philanthropist, and his distinguished wife, Clare Boothe Luce. They donated a large part of their estate to the monks in 1949. In 1993 the abbey church was completed, its Bell Tower of the Seven Spirits dedicated to "the voices of all who have lived on this land: American Indians, Laurens family, African-American slaves, Luce family, friends and relatives buried here, monastic community in glory, monastic community on the way."

Description: The approach to the abbey is an impressive, broad drive bordered on both sides by rows of ancient live oaks draped with Spanish moss. Deep in South Carolina's Low Country, the property sits along the banks of the Cooper River. The abbey is a place of wetlands and woodlands rich in varieties of flora and fauna.

Point of Interest: Historic Charleston is about an hour's drive from the abbey.

✤ TENNESSEE

St. Mary's Sewanee

P.O. Box 188, 770 St. Mary's Ln., Sewanee, TN 37375

Order: Affiliated with the Community of St. Mary (Episcopal)

Contact: Director

Telephone: 800-728-1659 or 931-598-5342. **Best time to call:** Mon. to Fri. 8 AM to 4 PM Central Time

Web site: www.stmaryssewanee.org; **e-mail:** stmaryscc@bellsouth.net

Accommodations: St. Mary's accommodates up to 105 guests, in single and double suites and a hermitage (private cabin). Four apartment/suites have private baths; the rest have shared baths.

Meals: Three meals daily

Costs: For single occupancy, room rates range from $26 (dormitory) to $58 (hermitage/private cabin). For double occupancy, room rates range from $38 to $80. For children under 12 in parent's room there is an additional fee of $10.50. Breakfast is $8.50, lunch is $9, and dinner is $12.75 ($10.75 for children 12 or younger).

Directions: From Nashville or Chattanooga, take I-24 and exit at the Monteagle/Sewanee exit. Turn toward the University of the South and Sewanee on US 41A. You will pass the TN 156 turnoff at St. Andrews, the University of the South turnoff, Sewanee Pharmacy, and Sewanee Market. Continue past all of these until you reach TN 56, then turn left toward Sherwood. Proceed about 1 mile on 56 to first major bend in road to left, and turn directly right onto St. Mary's Ln. This turn is marked with a sign reading "The Episcopal Church Welcomes You." Drive through stone pillars with cross on left. Continue until you reach gravel parking area on right. The office door has a sign reading "St. Mary's Episcopal Center."

Public Transportation: Groome Transportation provides shuttle service between Nashville and Chattanooga, with a stop at Monteagle/Exit 134

(reservation required); call 423-954-1400 or 800-896-9928 or visit www.groometransportation.com.

Description: St. Mary's is set high atop Tennessee's Cumberland Plateau, and guests may enjoy spectacular scenery from the windows of their rooms. This is a 200-acre property that is ruggedly beautiful and includes a pond, forests, rocky slopes, fields of wildflowers, and trails on which to explore them. St. Mary's is a secluded place with cool, green summers and vibrant autumn color, "a place made for reflection, renewal, relaxation, and thought."

Points of Interest: Just 2 miles down the road is the University of the South with its awe-inspiring Gothic Revival chapel. Seven state natural areas and parks are in the area, including Tims Ford. Other nearby sights include Hundred Oaks Castle, the Cowan Railroad Museum, Falls Mill, and the Old Jail Museum.

❖ TEXAS

Mount Carmel Center

4600 West Davis St., Dallas, TX 75211-3498

Order: Discalced Carmelite Friars (Roman Catholic)

Contact: Administrative Assistant

Telephone: 214-331-6224

Web site: www.mountcarmelcenter.org; **e-mail:** admin@mountcarmel center.org

Accommodations: Up to 18 guests (all men or all women) in single and double rooms, one of which has a private bath.

Meals: One cooked meal is served most days; refrigerated foods are available for other meals.

Costs: $45 per person per night

Directions: From I-30 take exit 39. Then take Cockrell south for 1.1 miles. Turn west onto Davis. Mount Carmel Center is on the south side, opposite the Vistas of Pinnacle Park.

Public Transportation: Contact administrative assistant for information.

History: The Discalced Carmelites began as a reform in 16th-century Spain, led by Saint Theresa of Avila and Saint John of the Cross. Mount Carmel Center was built in 1950.

Description: The center, built on 45 acres atop a hill, overlooks Dallas and the surrounding countryside. Guests may walk on the wooded grounds and use the large contemporary chapel as well as the smaller Byzantine oratory.

Points of Interest: Reunion Tower in Dallas offers views for miles in all directions. The Texas School Book Depository building is open to the public, and the city's monument to President John F. Kennedy is at John F. Kennedy Plaza. Old City Park is a museum of living history, where turn-of-the-20th-century homes, churches, and other buildings may be visited.

❖ UTAH

Abbey of Our Lady of the Holy Trinity
1250 South 9500 East, Huntsville, UT 84317

Order: Cistercian (Trappist) Monks (Roman Catholic)

Contact: Guest Master

Telephone: 801-745-3784 or 801-745-3931. Best times to call: 8 AM to noon and 2:30 PM to 5 PM Mountain Time

Web site: www.holytrinityabbey.org; **e-mail:** hta@xmission.com

Accommodations: Monastery accommodates up to 12 male guests, in single rooms, all with shared baths.

Meals: Three meals daily

Costs: "Voluntary offering"

Directions: From Salt Lake City or from points north, take I-15 to Ogden. Then take TX 39 East toward Huntsville. On 39, just before Huntsville and after the Texaco gas station on right, make right at monastery sign.

Public Transportation: There is air service to Salt Lake City International Airport (50 miles away). From airport and the city there is bus service to Huntsville's post office. Arrange in advance with guest master to be met at post office on arrival.

History: Originating in France in the 12th century, the Order of Cistercians of the Strict Observance (Trappists) have been in North America since 1848. Nearly a century later, in 1947, Trappist monks settled in Ogden Valley, an area "well suited to our needs for seclusion and beauty." Today the Utah community numbers nearly two dozen monks.

Description: Unique among monastic dwellings, Trinity Abbey is composed of a quadrangle of Quonset buildings, which the monks find "functional and adequate." Their farm includes 750 acres of irrigated fields producing barley, alfalfa, and wheat. The wheat is used in the monks' bakery in their whole-wheat and raisin breads. The farm also has about 300 beef cattle from which the monks sell calves and steers. Beyond the farm, the abbey has 1,100 acres of hill rangeland.

Special Note: The monks produce creamed honey and liquid honey, which they sell online, by mail order, and in the abbey store.

✣ VERMONT

Monastery of the Immaculate Heart of Mary

4103 Vermont Route 100, Westfield, VT 05874-7716

Order: Benedictine Nuns (Roman Catholic)

Contact: Guest Mistress

Telephone: 802-744-6525. Best times to call: 11 AM to noon and 3 PM to 5 PM Eastern Time

Web site: www.ihmwestfield.com; **e-mail:** monastery@ihmwestfield .com

Accommodations: Guest house accommodates three women, each in a single room, and all with shared baths. There is also one single-occupancy guest suite with private bath and study, which may be used by a priest or seminarian.

Meals: Three meals daily

Costs: The suggested donation is $35 per person per day for room and meals, $45 per person per day if staying in the suite.

Directions: From I-89 or I-91, take VT 100 to Westfield.

Public Transportation: There is air service to Burlington (two hours away), and bus service to Newport, Vermont (30 minutes away). From either arrival point, taxi or car rental is available.

History: The Benedictine Monastery of the Immaculate Heart of Mary traces its lineage to the 11th-century Abbey of Saint-Pierre de Solesmes, France. It was the great liturgist Dom Guéranger who restored monastic life to the monastery at Solesmes after the French Revolution. That was the beginning of the Congregation of Solesmes—part of the Benedictine family—which today has eight monasteries of nuns and 22 of monks in Europe, Africa, and the Americas. Nuns from the Abbaye Sainte-Marie des Deux-Montagnes (Canada) founded the Westfield monastery in 1981.

Description: Westfield is located in the beautiful Northeast Kingdom corner of Vermont. Here, one is surrounded by open fields, pine forests, deciduous trees, birds, deer, and other animals. The redbrick monastery is attractively designed with pitched roofs, bell towers, and windows that overlook scenes of nature's beauty. The abbey is traditional in many ways: the nuns' wearing of full monastic habit, their contemplative way of life, and their use of Latin Gregorian chant at church services. Seven times a day and once early in the morning, the bell tower calls the nuns to the monastery church to "sing the praise of the Lord."

Magna opera Domini; exquisita in omnes voluntates ejus.

The works of the Lord are great; sought out of all them that have pleasure therein.

—PSALM 111

Weston Priory

58 Priory Hill Rd., Weston, VT 05161

Order: Benedictine Monks (Roman Catholic)

Contact: Guest Brother

Telephone: 802-824-5409

Web site: www.westonpriory.org; **e-mail:** guestbrother@westonpriory.org

Accommodations: Romero House accommodates five men, each in a single room and all with shared bath. There are accommodations for five women in Morningside guest house, each in a single room and all with shared bath. In addition, there are accommodations for a group of up to eight adults in Bethany House.

Meals: Individual guests have three meals daily with the monks. Groups are requested to bring their own food and to prepare their meals in the kitchen at Bethany House.

Costs: "Freewill offering"

Directions: Take I-91 to Exit 6, then VT 103 west to Chester. Continue west about 3.5 miles; watch on right for sign to Andover and Weston. When you get to Weston Village, turn right onto VT 100 and continue north for 4 miles to junction of VT 155. Weston Priory is on first road to left north of VT 155.

Public Transportation: Priory Web site gives detailed information, or contact the guest brother.

History: A monk of Dormition Abbey in Jerusalem, Abbot Leo Rudloff, founded Weston Priory in 1953.

Description: The rustically simple monastery, chapels, guest houses, and other buildings are just outside the Green Mountain National Forest. The monks of Weston Priory have become widely known for their music and crafts. CDs, songbooks, and other items are for sale at the priory.

Points of Interest: Often called the prettiest village in Vermont, Weston is on the National Register of Historic Places. The Weston Playhouse is the oldest professional summer theater in Vermont. The Old Parish Church (1803) and the Church on the Hill are fine examples of 19th-century rural New England ecclesiastical architecture.

Special Note: The ordinary length of stay at the priory guest houses is from three to seven days. Reservations should be made at least four to six months in advance. Maps, brochures, and further information are available from the guest brother.

✤ VIRGINIA

Holy Cross Abbey

901 Cool Spring Ln., Berryville, VA 22611-2700

Order: Cistercian (Trappist) Monks (Roman Catholic)

Contact: Administrative Assistant

Telephone: 540-955-4383. Best times to call: 9 AM to noon, and 1 PM to 4:30 PM Eastern Time, weekdays only

Web site: www.hcava.org; **e-mail:** information@hcava.org

Accommodations: Guest house accommodates up to 15 individuals, each in a single room with private bath.

Meals: Three meals daily

Costs: "Suggested appropriate offering" for room and meals: for a weekend retreat (Fri. to Sat.), $150–$250, or for a weekday retreat (Mon. to Fri.), $200–$350. The offering is "according to your means," and "contributions are welcome from those who are able."

Directions: The abbey is 60 miles from Washington, D.C. Take VA 7 West across the Blue Ridge Mountains and Shenandoah River. Turn right on Route 603 immediately after crossing river.

Public Transportation: Contact administrative assistant for information.

History: Holy Cross Abbey is on a 1,200-acre estate formerly known as Cool Spring. The nucleus of the abbey is a stately hunting lodge built in 1784. The fields surrounding the lodge were the scene of a 1864 Civil War battle known as the Engagement. The monks acquired Cool Spring Estate in 1950.

Description: As it is so close to Washington, Holy Cross Abbey has aptly been described as "a capital escape." The 18th-century Cool Spring hunting lodge still dominates the land marked by the gently flowing Shenandoah River on one side and the majestic Blue Ridge Mountains on the other. The lodge has been supplemented with other buildings that form the abbey, among them the chapel, library, guest house, gift shop, and the monastery bakery, where the monks make Monastery Fruit Cake from "an old-fashioned, Southern recipe using choice fruits and nut meats in a brandy-laced batter."

Points of Interest: Berryville is in the Shenandoah Valley. The Shenandoah National Park and scenic Skyline Drive are just to the south. Belle Grove Plantation, an exceptional example of an 18th-century plantation house (now owned and open to the public by the National Trust) is in neighboring Middletown. The city of Winchester has a beautifully preserved cluster of 18th- and 19th-century homes, including one lived in by George Washington and another by Stonewall Jackson.

Mary Mother of the Church Abbey

12829 River Rd., Richmond, VA 23238

Order: Benedictine Monks (Roman Catholic)

Contact: Brother Jefferey, O.S.B., Guest Master

Telephone: 804-784-3509. **Best time to call:** 9 AM to 4 PM Eastern Time

Web site: www.richmondmonks.org; **e-mail:** brjefferey@richmond
monks.org

Accommodations: Retreat and Conference Center accommodates up to
54 guests in 27 twin-bedded rooms, some of which have private baths.

Meals: Three meals daily

Costs: $40 per person per day for room only. Breakfast is $6.25, lunch is
$8, and dinner is $9.75.

Directions: From I-64, take Exit 180-A. Drive onto Gaskins Rd. south. At
eighth traffic light, make right onto River Rd. Continue on River Rd. for
4.5 miles. Abbey will be on left.

Public Transportation: There is air, bus, and Amtrak service to Richmond.
Contact guest master for further information.

History: Founded in 1911, the community became an independent abbey
in 1989. The one dozen monks here pursue the Benedictine ideal of *ora et
labora* (prayer and work) at the abbey, in their parish, their high school,
and through chaplaincies.

Description: Protected by a field on one side and the historic James River
on the other, the abbey is a rambling modern structure. At its center is the
circular abbey church where the monks gather four times a day for services.

Points of Interest: Colonial Williamsburg is 60 miles south of Richmond.
En route are antebellum plantations that sit on the shores of the James
River, as does the abbey. The area also has a number of colonial Anglican
churches worth visiting. The history of Richmond, the state capital and
onetime capital of the Confederacy, is displayed in the Valentine Richmond

History Center. Among other sites, guests may visit the Jefferson-designed state capitol building, the Museum and White House of the Confederacy, and the Richmond National Battlefield Park.

✤ WASHINGTON

Holden Village
HCO Box 2, Chelan, WA 98816

Order: Affiliated with the Lutheran Church

Contact: Registrar

Telephone: 509-687-3644 (messages only)

Web site: www.holdenvillage.org; e-mail: registration@holdenvillage.org

Accommodations: Holden Village can accommodate up to 300 guests, in "comfortable but not elaborate lodging in two- and four-person rooms." Baths are shared.

Meals: Three meals daily. "Our family-style meals are simple, festive, and nutritious, with limited use of meat."

Costs: $71 per adult per day for room, meals, and transportation to and from Lucerne. Daily cost decreases with a longer stay. There are special rates for families with children.

Directions: Holden Village is above Lake Chelan in a remote part of north-central Washington State. From points east (including Spokane) or west (including Seattle), take US 2 to Wenatchee. Then drive north on US 97 to Chelan. You must park your car in Chelan (or preferably at Field Point) and then take a scenic boat ride to Lucerne. An 11-mile ride in a Holden vehicle completes the journey to Holden Village.

Public Transportation: There is air, train, and bus service to Wenatchee, and then bus service from Wenatchee to Chelan.

History: In response to the requests of a Lutheran lay worker, the Howe Sound Mining Company donated this former copper mining town in 1960. Since then many have generously supported Holden Village with their resources, talents, and time.

Description: Holden Village is gloriously situated in a valley winding through the glacial peaks and alpine lakes of Wenatchee National Forest in the North Cascades, offering ample opportunities for hiking, climbing, and fishing. Interestingly, the village is an abandoned mining town in the wilderness, its buildings now used as a library, bookstore, museum, pottery shop, post office, snack bar, pool hall, bowling alley, and Hike Haus. There are also a sauna and a Jacuzzi.

Points of Interest: Holden Village is above the shores of Lake Chelan, a 55-mile-long lake with some of the most pristine waters in America. The lake lies within an 80-mile-long glacial valley that includes portions of a National Park, two National Forest Wilderness areas, and a National Recreation area.

Special Note: "At Holden, you join people of diverse backgrounds and interests . . . couples, families, and singles . . . young and old in a welcoming place of grace and renewal."

Kairos House of Prayer

W. 1714 Stearns Rd., Spokane, WA 99208

Order: Roman Catholic

Contact: Rita Beaulieu or Sister Florence Leone

Telephone: 509-466-2187. **Best time to call:** midmorning to midafternoon, Pacific Time.

Accommodations: The main house, barn loft, and eight hermitages serve up to 15 guests in single rooms.

Meals: Three meals daily (vegetarian)

Costs: $35 per person per day for room and meals. "That no one be denied a Kairos time because of finances, please inquire about reductions prior to coming."

Directions: From I-90, take Exit 281 (Newport-Colvill) and then drive north on US 2/395 (Division St.). Continue straight on US 395 and take the Wandermere Rd. exit. Pass Wandermere Golf Course. Take first left (Dartford Dr.) to Kairos House of Prayer.

Public Transportation: Take Spokane Transit Authority bus to Hastings, which is about 2 miles from Kairos. Arrange in advance for pickup on arrival.

History: The first pioneers arrived in this area around 1807 and settled along the banks of the Spokane River. These were fur trappers and traders. Later, they were followed by missionaries who came to the region to work among the Native American population. Spokane Falls (as the town was originally named) has grown to today's Spokane, the Lilac City. It is the largest city between Minneapolis and San Francisco.

Description: Kairos, an ecumenical house open to all, is on 27 acres of beautiful meadows and forested hillside. The main living facility includes a large room that serves as a chapel and a place of meditation. For those seeking greater solitude, the hermitages are scattered farther afield on the wooded property.

Points of Interest: The area north of Spokane has mountains, lakes, rivers, forests, craters, canyons, ghost towns, and dams. Fifty miles east of Spokane is the Old Mission at Cataldo, Idaho, built in 1850–53 by the Coeur d'Alene Indian tribe and Catholic missionaries.

St. Placid Priory
Spirituality Center

500 College St. NE, Lacey, WA 98516

Order: Benedictine Sisters (Roman Catholic)

Contact: Sr. Lucy Wynkoop or Carolyn Galloway

Telephone: 360-438-2595. **Best time to call:** Mon. to Fri., 9 AM to 4 PM Pacific Time

Web site: www.stplacid.org; **e-mail:** spiritualitycenter@stplacid.org

Accommodations: Guest house accommodates up to 19 individuals.

Meals: Three meals daily

Costs: $40 to $70 per person per day for room and meals

Directions: Visit Web site or contact priory for map and driving directions.

Public Transportation: There is Greyhound bus and Amtrak rail service to Lacey. Contact priory in advance for pickup on arrival.

History: St. Placid was founded a half-century ago, and for many years the sisters staffed a high school. Moving to their present home in 1992, they now serve the wider, ecumenical community with their ministry at the Spirituality Center.

Description: The priory is a contemporary wooden building beautifully situated in a clearing in the woods. The interior is spacious and well furnished and has a chapel, library, and gift store. Guests are welcome to explore the surrounding nature trails and to visit the meditation gazebo.

Points of Interest: The priory is near many of Washington's natural attractions: the Olympic Peninsula, Puget Sound, Mount Rainier National Park, Mount St. Helens National Volcanic Monument, rainforests, and ocean beaches. Olympia, the state's capital, is also close by.

Special Note: The center also offers "programs, including training for spiritual direction and ministries of healing touch and massage."

✤ WISCONSIN

Holy Hill

1525 Carmel Rd., Hubertus, WI 53033

Order: Discalced Carmelite Friars (Roman Catholic)

Contact: Reservations Office

Telephone: 262-628-1838, ext. 127

Web site: www.holyhill.com; **e-mail:** KarenGirard@holyhill.com

Accommodations: The New Guest House has 14 rooms, each with twin beds for single or double occupancy use, and each with a private bath. In addition, 15 guests may be accommodated in the Old Monastery Inn, each in a single room and all with shared baths.

Meals: Guests are welcome to prepare their own meals in the New Guest House kitchen, or they may dine in the Holy Hill Café (hours vary by season) or any of the area restaurants.

Costs: $35 per room per night, single occupancy, plus sales tax; $45 per room per night, double occupancy, plus sales tax.

Directions: Holy Hill is 30 miles north of Milwaukee. Take I-94 to US 45 North. Exit onto WI 167 West and drive for 6 miles. Entrance and sign will be on left.

Public Transportation: No public transportation to Holy Hill.

History: Early in the 13th century a small group of European hermits settled on Mount Carmel in the Holy Land. Building a chapel there dedicated to the Virgin, they were known as the Brothers of Our Lady of Mount Carmel, or more popularly as Carmelites. The Carmelites flourished in Europe. In 16th-century Spain, Saint Theresa of Avila and Saint John of the Cross established a separate, more contemplative branch of the order. They chose to wear sandals as poor folk did at that time, and so they became known as barefoot, or discalced, Carmelites. Although Discalced Carmelite friars accompanied early Spanish explorers of California, they did not make a permanent foundation in North America until 1906, when Bavarian friars came to Wisconsin. There they built the National Shrine of Mary, Help of Christians, which in its centenary year was elevated to the status of a basilica.

Description: Listed on the National Register of Historic Places, Holy Hill is crowned by a massive neo-Romanesque church, its interior embellished with mosaics and priceless German stained-glass windows. Guests can visit the outdoor Stations of the Cross, the Lourdes grotto, and more secluded spots on the 435-acre property, which is crossed by Wisconsin's Ice Age Trail. There is a flight of 178 steps leading to the top of the church's tower. Those who venture up are rewarded with unrivaled panoramas of the surrounding countryside and the Milwaukee skyline on the horizon.

> *O send out thy light and thy truth, that they may lead me,*
> *and bring me unto thy holy hill, and to thy dwelling.*
>
> —PSALM 43

Holy Wisdom Monastery

4200 County Highway M, Middleton, WI 53582-2317

Order: Benedictine Sisters (Ecumenical)

Contact: Monastery Receptionist

Telephone: 608-836-1631, ext. 101. **Best time to call:** 8:30 AM to 4 PM Central Time

Web site: www.benedictinewomen.org; **e-mail:** info@bendictinewomen.org

Accommodations: Monastery accommodates up to 21 guests, in 13 single and four twin-bedded rooms, each with private bath.

Meals: Continental breakfast daily; lunch and dinner Tues. through Sat.

Costs: $47 per person for an overnight stay and continental breakfast. $33 per person for a day room only. Lunch and dinner are $5.50 and $7, respectively.

Directions: The monastery is on the northwest side of Lake Mendota, just outside Madison. From the Chicago area, take I-90 north to WI 30 West (Exit 138-B). Follow WI 30 to the exit for WI 113 4 miles to the junction with County Road M. Turn left on M. It is then 4 miles to monastery.

From Milwaukee, take I-94 West to just outside Madison, where I-94 becomes WI 30. Follow WI 30 to WI 113 North as above.

Public Transportation: There is air service to Dane County Regional Airport in Madison, where car rental is available. Both Greyhound and Badger have bus service to Madison. From the bus station it is a 7.5-mile taxi ride to the monastery.

History: This was the first ecumenical monastic community of women in America.

Description: On 130 acres of rolling countryside, Holy Wisdom Monastery includes a 10,000-year-old glacial lake, a newly created wetland, wooded nature trails, prairie areas, orchards, and gardens. In 2009 a new monastery building was opened. The monastery and its surroundings are designed to reflect Benedictine values and principles and "incorporate 'green' elements in its every aspect."

> *Wisdom hath builded her an house . . .*
>
> —PROVERBS 9:1

Mary's Margin

S83 W27815 Beaver Trail, Mukwonago, WI 53149

Order: Sisters of St. Mary (Episcopal)

Contact: Guest Mistress

Telephone: 262-363-8489. **Best time to call:** 9 AM to 7 PM Central Time

Web site: www.marysmargin.com; **e-mail:** info@marysmargin.com

Accommodations: Houses two guests in single rooms and two in the hermitage

Meals: Three meals daily

Costs: Suggested fee is $60 per day

Directions: From Milwaukee, take I-43 south. Make a right onto WI 164, then a left on County Rd. ES and a right on Hillview (this will be the second right after County Rd. XX). Then make a left on Whitetail and a right on Beaver Trail to the driveway at end of road.

Public Transportation: Contact guest mistress for information.

History: The Community of St. Mary, the oldest religious community in the Episcopal Church, was founded in New York City in 1865. It was in 1904 that their Western Province, based in Wisconsin, was begun. A "margin" is the open space surrounding a printed page. So, too, it can mean any border or edge. "The name is both geographically and spiritually apt. Mary's Margin is on the edge of a subdivision and of the Vernon Marsh. It is also a place for spiritual exploration and discernment. It is a space where people can get outside the story of their lives and edit it."

Description: On four acres in beautifully wooded hills overlooking the Fox River Valley, Mary's Margin has an enchanting little chapel. The house includes a comfortable great room that overlooks a picturesque marsh. The sisters have created a labyrinth with paths through the woods, which end at a 16-foot tower overlooking the Vernon Wildlife Marsh.

The DeKoven Center

600 21st St., Racine, WI 53403

Order: Episcopal

Contact: Facilities Coordinator

Telephone: 262-633-6401

Web site: www.dekovencenter.org; **e-mail:** info@dekovencenter.org

Accommodations: "Capacity is 60–70 people in 32 guest rooms. Six rooms are singles. We make triples out of some of the larger doubles to meet capacity for larger groups. The bathrooms are shared and gender-specific."

Meals: There is full meal service for groups only. "Individuals may 'piggy-back' on group meals to use our guest refrigerator and microwave."

Costs: "Interested parties should call for rates."

Directions: From I-94, exit onto WI 11 (this is the first Racine exit coming north from Chicago, and the last Racine exit coming south from Milwaukee). Take WI 11 to end, where you'll see the Case Tractor sign. Make a left onto WI 32/Racine St. Then turn right onto 21st St. DeKoven Center is at 21st and Lake Michigan. Once on property, follow the signs.

Public Transportation: Amtrak has rail service from Chicago to Racine, and Metra/Union Pacific District North Line has rail service from Chicago to Kenosha. Wisconsin Coach Lines has shuttle service from O'Hare and Midway airports, and daily commuter service among Racine, Kenosha, and downtown Milwaukee. Racine Yellow Cab is at 262-634-2222.

History: The DeKoven Center is one of the most architecturally significant places in the Midwest. Its nine Gothic Revival buildings served as Racine College from 1852 to 1876. James DeKoven, an Episcopal priest, was the warden of Racine College.

Description: Beautifully sited on 11 wooded acres along the shore of Lake Michigan, the DeKoven Center's cream-colored buildings form a quadrangle, very English in appearance. The guest house, Taylor Hall, was built in 1867 as housing for Racine College faculty and students. The hall has elegant common rooms furnished and decorated with antiques. Other buildings include the Great Hall (which resembles an English boarding-school refectory), the historic St. John's Chapel (which is lighted by Belgian stained-glass windows), and the indoor swimming pool (the oldest in the Midwest, featuring mosaic tiles and large windows facing the quad-rangle).

✥ WYOMING

San Benito Monastery

P.O. Box 520, 859 Main St., Dayton, WY 82836

Order: Benedictine Sisters of Perpetual Adoration (Roman Catholic)

Contact: Guest Mistress

Telephone: 307-655-9013. Best times to call: 9 AM to noon and 2 PM to 5 PM Mountain Time

Web site: www.benedictinesisters.org; **e-mail:** sanbenito@trcable.tv

Accommodations: Mobile home on monastery grounds accommodates three guests in single rooms, all with shared bath, living room, and kitchen/dining room.

Meals: Three meals daily: breakfast in the mobile home and two meals with the community

Costs: $25 per person per night

Directions: From I-90 take US 14 and drive through Rochester to Dayton. On the way out of Dayton, going toward the mountains, you will see a small blue sign at the end of a small bridge with the monastery house number, 858. Turn left on that road. The monastery, a cluster of blue buildings, is at the end of the road.

Public Transportation: United Airlines has service to Sheridan. Arrange in advance with the guest mistress to be met on arrival.

History: The Benedictine Sisters of Perpetual Adoration was founded amid the rolling hills of northwest Missouri in 1874. San Benito Monastery was opened in 1983. The sisters help support themselves by baking and selling altar breads.

Description: San Benito Monastery is a village of blue houses on 38 acres of woodland and cleared fields. The Big Horn Mountains can clearly be seen from San Benito.

Points of Interest: Dayton has some of the largest cattle ranches in the world. On many summer weekends there are rodeo events in the area.

This corner of Wyoming, the Equality State, is known for its historic sites, Native American culture, and cowboy folklore. From the monastery it is a short drive to the Big Horn Mountains and to Tongue River Canyon.

CANADA

❖ MANITOBA

Our Lady of the Prairies Abbey

P .O. Box 310, Holland, MB R0G 0X0

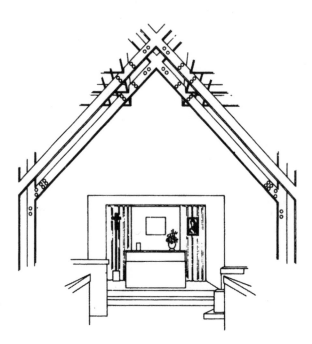

Order: Cistercian (Trappist) Monks (Roman Catholic)

Contact: Guest Master

Telephone: 204-526-2000

Accommodations: Monastery accommodates four guests in single rooms with private baths; guest house serves an additional four individuals, in single rooms with shared baths.

Meals: Three meals daily

Costs: $30 per person per day for room and meals

Directions: From Winnipeg, take Route 2 West to Holland, a two-hour drive.

Public Transportation: There is air service to Winnipeg. Contact guest master for additional information.

History: The Abbey of Bellefontaine, France, founded Notre-Dame des Prairies in 1892. Initially located in St. Norbert, a suburb of Winnipeg, the community moved to Holland in 1978 "in order to regain the solitude necessary to monastic life."

Description: Our Lady of the Prairies Abbey is in an agricultural setting surrounded by rolling hills and clusters of tall, old trees. Occasionally, groups of deer may be seen grazing not far from the monastery and guest house.

Points of Interest: Spruce Woods Park is near the abbey. Also close by, in the town of Austin, is the Manitoba Agricultural Museum. The museum has a permanent installation of "prairie giants" (antique tractors and threshing machines). Visitors may also see the re-creation of an 1800s homesteaders' village of log homes, a church, and a school.

St. Benedict's Monastery
Retreat and Conference Centre

225 Masters Ave., Winnipeg, MB R4A 2A1

Order: Benedictine Sisters (Roman Catholic)

Contact: Guest Mistress

Telephone: 204-339-1705. **Best time to call:** 8:30 AM to 4 PM Central Time

Web site: www.stbens.ca; **e-mail:** stbenscentre@mts.net

Accommodations: Retreat and Conference Centre can serve up to 55 guests. One room has a double bed; the others have two twin beds. Six of the rooms have private bath; the others have shared baths.

Meals: Three meals daily

Costs: Contact monastery for current charges.

Directions: Perimeter Highway 101 encircles Winnipeg. Take Highway 9 north of Perimeter Highway 101. Go 3 kilometers (just under 2 miles) on Highway 9. Just after a large curve in the highway you will see a sign for the monastery. Turn right on Masters Ave. First drive on left leads to Retreat and Conference Centre entrance.

Public Transportation: From the Winnipeg bus terminal take the Beaver Bus that goes to Selkirk; ask to be let off at St. Benedict's. It is a five-minute walk up Masters Ave. to St. Benedict's.

History: Four Benedictine sisters from Minnesota arrived in Winnipeg in 1912 with the mission of "education and the practice of Christian charity." They opened an orphanage and schools. In 1961 the monastery was moved from the city to its present rural spot. The Retreat and Conference Centre opened here in 1970. Today the community numbers 25 sisters who are dedicated to hospitality, spiritual formation, and education.

Description: St. Benedict's has 72 wooded acres situated along the banks of the Red River. Guests are welcome to walk the paths and the seasonal labyrinth, or to ride their bicycles along the monastery's bicycle path.

Points of Interest: Winnipeg has many cultural institutions, including the Royal Winnipeg Ballet, Manitoba Theatre Centre, Winnipeg Symphony Orchestra, the Manitoba Opera, and the Manitoba Museum. The city also hosts cultural festivals, some of which reflect its diverse ethnic background.

Special Note: "We are pleased to offer space where you can find rest and renewal."

❖ NEW BRUNSWICK

Abbaye Notre-Dame de l'Assomption
Rogersville, NB E4Y 2W8

Order: Cistercian (Trappistine) Nuns (Roman Catholic)

Contact: Guest Mistress

Telephone: 506-775-2322

Web site: www.trappistine.org; **e-mail:** abbey@nb.aibn.com

Accommodations: Guest wing of monastery houses seven women, in single rooms, all with shared baths.

Meals: Three meals daily

Costs: Suggested donation of $35 per person per day for room and meals

Directions: Take Trans-Canada Highway to Route 126 (from Moncton going toward Miramichi).

Public Transportation: VIA Rail Canada (on route between Halifax and Montreal) stops in Rogersville. Contact guest mistress for additional information and directions.

History: The Cistercian nuns date back to 12th-century France. This particular community was founded in Lyons, France, in 1820, moved to Canada in 1904, and was raised to the status of an abbey in 1927.

Description: The abbey church is in the midst of farm fields and forests of pine and birch trees. The nuns provide for their basic needs through the baking and sale of altar breads. The community is bilingual (speaking French and English) and its liturgy is in French.

Special Note: "The abbey guest house welcomes people seeking to make silent retreats." This is a smoke-free environment. Reservations are necessary.

J'ai demande l'hospitalite et vous m'avez recu.

I was a stranger, and ye took me in.

—MATTHEW 25:35

Our Lady of Calvary Abbey

11505 Route 126, Rogersville, NB E0A 2T0

Order: Cistercian (Trappist) Monks (Roman Catholic)

Contact: Father Abbot

Telephone: 506-775-2331

Web site: www.calvaryabbey.com; **e-mail:** Bedeabb@aol.com

Accommodations: Guest house accommodates 11, in single and twin-bedded rooms, two of which have private baths.

Meals: Three meals daily

Costs: Suggested donation of $40 to $70 per person day for room and meals

Directions: From Moncton, New Brunswick, take Route 126 North. Monastery is 3 miles north of the Rogersville Catholic Church.

Public Transportation: VIA Rail Canada has passenger service to Rogersville. Arrange in advance to be met on arrival.

History: In 1902 six monks from the Abbey of Bonnecombe, France, arrived in New Brunswick. They wished to found a "farming monastic community," acquiring an old farm that had a house, farm buildings, a sawmill, and a gristmill. The monastery became an independent abbey in 1960. The work of the monks remains agricultural; they raise cows and chickens. The monks also produce and sell pottery to help support themselves.

Description: The nucleus of the abbey is a large stone building surrounded by fields and woodland. Visitors may wish to visit the abbey's Lourdes Grotto.

Cannot I do with you as this potter? saith the Lord.
Behold, as the clay is in the potter's hand, so are ye in
mine hand . . .

—JEREMIAH 18:6

❖ NOVA SCOTIA

Bethany Place
P.O. Box 762, Digby, NS B0V 1A0

Order: Society of Our Lady Saint Mary (Anglican Church of Canada)

Contact: Sister Bonnie, S.L.S.M.

Telephone: 902-245-4841. **Best time to call:** between 9 AM and 9 PM Atlantic Time

Accommodations: Hermitage accommodates one guest; guest cottage houses one or two guests.

Meals: None

Costs: Suggested donation of $280 per week for the hermitage, and $450 per week for the guest cottage

Directions: From Maine, enter Nova Scotia at Yarmouth via ferry service from Bar Harbor. From Yarmouth, take Highway 101 East to Digby, then take Highway 217 West to Rossway. Bethany Place is House 10275.

There is daily ferry service (the *Princess of Acadia*) from Saint John, New Brunswick, directly to Digby. Once disembarked, take Highway 217 West to Rossway.

From Halifax, Nova Scotia, take Highway 101 West to Digby. At Digby, take Highway 217 west to Digby Neck and Islands and to Rossway.

Public Transportation: There is transportation service to Digby from Halifax and from Yarmouth, Nova Scotia. Arrange in advance to be met on arrival.

History: The Society of Our Lady Saint Mary has been in Nova Scotia since 1979. The sisters at Bethany Place live a life of prayer and apostolic outreach.

Description: The hermitage is just beyond the sisters' house, 20 miles west of Digby in the quaint fishing village of Sandy Cove. Guests may enjoy visits to the beaches. There are also hiking trails in the area. Whale watching is a favorite local pastime.

Points of Interest: In 1605 the French made the first permanent European settlement in the area at Port Royal. Known today as Annapolis Royal, this is one of the many historic sites, steepled villages, beaches, coves, and picturesque tree-lined towns one sees while touring the coastal drive of Nova Scotia. An interesting aside: while Nova Scotia is famed for its seafood (lobster, oysters, shrimps, clams, and crabs), Digby lends its name to the famed Digby scallop.

Special Note: The cottage is open from the beginning of May until mid-October; the hermitage is available year round.

❖ ONTARIO

Crieff Hills Community
RR#2, Puslinch, ON N0B 2J0

Order: Crieff Hills Community (Presbyterian Church in Canada)

Contact: Registrar

Telephone: 519-824-7898 or 1-800-884-1525

Web site: www.crieffhills.com; **e-mail:** infor@crieffhills.com

Accommodations: Seven guest houses accommodate up to 100 individuals, in twin and single rooms, some with private baths. Additional personal retreat space was in the planning stage at time of writing.

Meals: In some guest houses, meals are provided; in others meals are self-catered.

Costs: Contact registrar for current rates

Directions: Crieff Hills is 3 kilometers (just under 2 miles) south of Highway 401, 5 kilometers (3.1 miles) west of Highway 6 (on Leslie Rd.), and 10 kilometers (6.2 miles) east of Cambridge Townline Rd. (on Puslinch Rd. 1).

Public Transportation: Airways Transit has service from Toronto International Airport to Cambridge Holiday Inn. In addition, there is bus and train service to Guelph. Contact registrar for more information.

History: Crieff is named after a town at the edge of the Scottish Highlands. Scots settled here in the 1830s to clear the land and build log cabins and barns. These, in time, were replaced with stone dwellings. In the 1920s Colonel John B. MacLean (founder of *MacLean's* magazine and the *Financial Post*) restored the church grounds, was given the old manse, and acquired adjacent land, which he named Crieff Hills Farm. When he died in 1950, he left this to the Presbyterian Church in Canada. In the 1970s the farm was developed into a retreat center.

Description: Crieff Hills has 250 acres of rolling farmland with charming and picturesque old stone and wood buildings, converted for use by the community and its guests. Among these 11 buildings are a squared log house (1838), a stone house (1872), a stone schoolhouse (1874), and a delightful old milk house.

Points of Interest: Located in south-central Ontario, Crieff Hills is within easy access to Niagara Falls and Toronto.

Holy Cross Priory

204 High Park Ave., Toronto, ON M6P 2S6

Order: Order of the Holy Cross (Anglican Church of Canada)

Contact: Prior

Telephone: 416-767-9081. Best times to call: 8:30 AM to noon, and 5:30 PM to 6:30 PM Eastern Time

Web site: www.ohc-canada.org

Accommodations: Priory accommodates four guests in single and double rooms, all with shared baths.

Meals: Breakfast only. Other meals by special arrangement.

Costs: $60 per person per day for bed and breakfast. Additional meals are negotiable.

Directions: Contact the prior for driving directions and information on public transportation.

History: In 1884 the Order of the Holy Cross was founded in New York City by an Episcopal priest, James Otis Sargent Huntington. The order's earliest charitable works were on New York's Lower East Side. In the century following, the monks made other foundations in North America and West Africa. "In slum and suburb, rain forest and city, illiterate tribesmen and sophisticated Westerners alike have shared the word of God with the monks of the Holy Cross." In 1973 the monks came to Toronto and moved to their present home in 1984.

Description: The priory is a handsome three-story Queen Anne–style red-brick house, complete with wraparound porch with classical columns, and a corner tower topped with a turret.

Points of Interest: Toronto, Canada's largest city and Ontario's provincial capital, sits on the shores of Lake Ontario. The 1,800-foot-high CN Tower offers sweeping views of both lake and city. Closer to ground, visitors may explore Toronto's religious, historical, and cultural sites. The city also has several professional sports teams.

Monastery of Mount Carmel

7021 Stanley Ave., Niagara Falls, ON L2G 7B7

Order: Carmelite Friars (Roman Catholic)

Contact: Director

U.S. mailing address: P.O. Box 767, Niagara Falls, NY 14302-0767

Telephone: 905-356-4113. **Best time to call:** 8:30 AM to 5 PM, Mon. to Fri. Eastern Time

Web site: www.carmelniagara.com; **e-mail:** mtcarmel@carmelniagara .com

Accommodations: Monastery houses up to 82 guests in 41 double rooms, each with private bath; guest house (annex) accommodates an additional 18 guests in single rooms all with shared baths.

Meals: Three meals daily

Costs: Contact monastery for current charges

Directions: From Toronto, take Queen Elizabeth Way (QEW) to McLeod Rd. exit (Exit 27). Turn left on Stanley Ave. Monastery will be on right. Enter at second driveway.

From Buffalo area, take I-90 and Robert Moses Parkway North. Turn right at sign reading "To Falls" and "Bridge to Canada." Continue straight onto John B. Daly Parkway. Turn left at T intersection (Niagara St.). Rainbow Bridge to Canada will be straight ahead. After Immigration and Customs Canada, follow signs to Highway 420. Turn left on Stanley Ave. (at second traffic light). Drive 5 kilometers (3 miles) to monastery, which will be on left.

Public Transportation: Contact monastery for information.

History: The friars of the Order of the Brothers of the Blessed Virgin Mary, or Carmelites, as they are popularly known, came to Niagara Falls in 1875. At first they lived in a simple farmhouse. In 1894 they built the present monastery, and the main chapel was added in 1926.

Description: The massive monastery and chapel are solid granite buildings. The "Main Chapel possesses a unique beauty because of its monastic simplicity." Its interior is lit with English and Canadian stained-glass windows, and the hand-carved woodwork is American white oak stained a seal brown. This is one of four chapels on the 12-acre property, which has gardens, wooded areas, and open spaces. The monastery enjoys a site overlooking Niagara Falls. An indoor labyrinth is a copy of that in the 12th-century Chartres Cathedral. A gift shop and bookstore are also here.

Points of Interest: Niagara Falls is on the Niagara River midway between two of the Great Lakes: Lake Ontario and Lake Erie. While it may possibly be the world's best-known falls, Niagara Falls is certainly the most visited, with an annual visitation of about 14 million people. Queen Victoria Park stretches along the banks of the Niagara River and is planted with beautiful gardens. The falls may also be seen from observation towers or by boat. (Hooded raincoats are provided!)

Special Note: Classical music concerts are performed in the Main Chapel Sunday afternoons at 2 PM.

St. John's Convent

233 Cummer Ave., Toronto, ON M2M 2E8

Order: Sisterhood of St. John the Divine (Anglican Church of Canada)

Contact: Guest House Administrator

Telephone: 416-226-2201, ext. 305. **Best time to call:** Tues. to Fri. 9 AM to 4:30 PM Eastern Time

Web site: www.ssjd.ca; **e-mail:** guesthouse@ssjd.ca

Accommodations: Guest house accommodates up to 40 individuals, in 32 single rooms with shared baths and four double rooms with private baths.

Meals: Three meals daily. ("No food is allowed to be brought in from the outside.")

Costs: $50 per person per night for bed and breakfast ($40 for students and seniors); $70 per person per night for single room and three meals ($60 for students and seniors); $80 per person per night for double en suite room and three meals ($70 for students and seniors).

Directions: Take Highway 401 to Bayview exit. Take Bayview Ave. northbound. Drive about 3 kilometers (just under 2 miles) to Cummer Ave. Turn left on Cummer and continue about 1 kilometer (less than a mile). Convent is on left, just past entrance to St. John's Rehab Hospital. Pull into convent drive and turn left after chapel; stop at front door. Ring bell (right of post), enter vestibule, and wait for someone to greet you.

Public Transportation: Take the Toronto Transit system subway (Yonge St. line) north to Finch Station (last stop on line). Then take Cummer 42 bus to stop outside Cummer Lodge and Willowdale Manor (i.e., first stop after Willowdale Ave.). Walk east a half block to convent driveway and ring bell as above.

History: The Sisterhood of St. John the Divine is the only Anglican religious order of women founded in Canada. It was begun in 1884 in Toronto. Sixty years later the sisters moved to Willowdale, and at the start of the 21st century moved to their present home on Cummer Avenue. The Sisterhood has worked in all five Canadian provinces.

Description: The convent is in a quiet residential area of North Toronto. It is a modern facility and is fully handicapped accessible. The grounds include a labyrinth for walking meditation.

Points of Interest: Metropolitan Toronto offers many cultural attractions, including the Royal Ontario Museum and other museums, the Casa Loma, the Ontario Parliament building, and the CN Tower.

Special Note: "St. John's Convent Guest House is a quiet place apart, where people from all over Canada and beyond come to pray, meditate, and find spiritual nurture. We can help you reconnect with yourself, with others, and with God."

❖ QUEBEC

Abbaye Saint-Benoît-du-Lac
Saint-Benoît-du-Lac, QC J0B 2M0

Order: Benedictine Monks (Roman Catholic)

Contact: Men: Père Hôtelier (Guest Master); Women: contact villa (see Special Note below)

Telephone: 819-843-4080. Best times to call: 8:30 AM to 10:30 AM and 3 PM to 4:40 PM Eastern Time

Web site: www.st-benoit-du-lac.com; **e-mail:** abbaye@st-benoit-du-lac.com

Accommodations: Abbey houses up to 30 men and 15 women in separate facilities, each in single rooms and all with shared baths

Meals: Three meals daily

Costs: Suggested donation of $50 per person per day for room and meals

Directions: From the New York or New England areas, take I-89 North from Burlington, Vermont, toward St. Albans to Route 105. Continue on 105 East to Richford. Then pick up Route 243 until it merges with Route 245. Continue on to Bolton Center. You will then see signs directing you to abbey.

From points east (Quebec City) or west (Montreal) on Autoroute 10, change to Route 112 (Exit 116) and then pick up Chemin des Pères. Continue south on Chemin des Pères until you arrive in Austin, where there are signs directing you to abbey.

Public Transportation: Contact guest master for information.

History: Monks from Normandy, France, arrived in southern Quebec in 1912 to found Saint-Benoît-du-Lac. The present buildings were started in 1939 and designed by Dom Paul Bellot, a noted French monk and architect. The abbey guest house was completed in 1962, and the church in 1994.

Description: The buildings at St.-Benoît can best be described as French Gothic Revival with strong borrowings from Moorish architecture. Throughout, dominant features include high-pitched roofs, lancet windows, and a permanent polychrome in brick and tile. Surrounding the massive abbey are the wonders of nature: a truly bucolic setting of thick forests (ablaze with color in autumn), fields, the serene Lake Memphremagog, and the mountains beyond. The monks of St.-Benoît are known for their Gregorian chant, and they support themselves by producing cheeses, apple sauce, and apple cider. These foods and CDs of the monks' singing are sold at the abbey shop (open from 9 AM to 10:30 AM and from noon to 4:30 PM).

Points of Interest: Montreal is 140 kilometers (90 miles) west of the abbey, offering cathedrals, churches, and other points of historic and cultural interest.

Special Note: Men are accommodated at the abbey guest house (Hôtellerie Monastique). Women are housed at the Villa Ste-Scholastique, also on the grounds of the abbey.

> *He saith unto them, Come and see.*
>
> —JOHN 1:39

Abbaye Sainte-Marie des Deux-Montagnes

2803 Chemin d'Oka, Ste.-Marthe-sur-le-Lac, QC J0N 1P0

Order: Benedictine Nuns (Roman Catholic)

Contact: Guest Sister

Telephone: 450-473-7278

Web site: abbsainte-mariedm.com

Accommodations: Abbey accommodates six women, in four single and one twin-bedded room, all with shared bath.

Meals: Three meals daily

Costs: $50 per person per day for room and meals

Directions: Abbey is 30 minutes from Montreal. Take Autoroute 15 or 13 North to 640 West, then take Exit 8 to Deux-Montagnes (20th Ave.). On the Chemin d'Oka turn right and drive 1 mile.

Public Transportation: There is air service to Montreal Dorval Airport. There is rail service from Central Station to the Deux-Montagnes city station. From the station there is taxi service to abbey.

History: At the invitation of the Archbishop of Montreal, four nuns from the Monastery of Notre-Dame de Wisques, France, came to Canada in 1936 to open a monastery. In 10 years' time the monastery had grown so that it was raised to the status of abbey, and the foundress, Mother Gertrude Adam, was solemnly blessed as the first abbess. This is a monastery of the Congregation of Solesmes.

Description: The abbey, surrounded by fields and trees, is an extensive redbrick building, embellished with polychrome brickwork, towers, and spires. The architect was Edgar Courchesne, the Canadian disciple of Dom Paul Bellot, the "brick poet" who greatly influenced monastic and ecclesiastic architecture in Europe and America. A traditional monastic community, the nuns have preserved the use of Latin Gregorian chant in the great abbey church, recordings of which may be purchased by mail or in the abbey shop. The abbey has an excellent bookbindery, and the nuns also paint icons, print cards, and make rosaries. "Being cloistered nuns with papal enclosure," they "wish to bear witness to the rich heritage from Solesmes and also share it with guests and visitors."

Point of Interest: The abbey is near the Lac des Deux Montagnes, named for the last two mountains of the Laurentides.

> *Laetatus sum in his que dicta sunt mihi:*
> *In domum Domini ibimus.*
>
> *I rejoiced at this that was said unto me:*
> *We shall go into the house of the Lord.*
>
> —PSALM 119

Abbaye Val Notre-Dame

250 Chemin de la Montagne-Coupée, Saint-Jean-de-Matha,
QC J0K 2S0

Order: Cistercian (Trappist) Monks (Roman Catholic)

Contact: Guest Master

Telephone: 450-960-2889, ext. 1164

Web site: www.abbayevalnotredame.ca; **e-mail:** communaute@abbaye
valnotredame.ca

Accommodations: Guest house accommodates up to 13 individuals in
single rooms, all with shared baths.

Meals: Three meals daily

Costs: Suggested donation of $45 per person per day for room and meals

Directions: From Montreal, take Autoroute 40 East to Route 131 North to
Joliette. Continue on Route 131, driving through the town of Saint-Félix-
de-Valois. Make a left on Chemin de la Montagne-Coupée. Monastery will
be on left.

Public Transportation: Contact guest master for information.

History: In 1881 seven monks from the Abbey of Bellefontaine, France, established this, the first Trappist community in Canada. They in turn have
founded two other Canadian monasteries. In 2009 the monks moved to
their new home in Saint-Jean-de-Matha.

Description: The abbey, a strikingly modern design built of masonry and
wood, is in a beautiful, tranquil setting.

Auberge de la Basilique

5 Rue Règina, Sainte-Anne-de-Beaupré, QC G0A 3C0

Order: Redemptorist Fathers (Roman Catholic)

Contact: Reception Staff

Telephone: 418-827-5162. Best times to call: Mon. to Fri., Nov. to Apr., 9 AM to 4 PM, and May to Oct. 7 AM to 11 PM Eastern Time

Web site: www.ssadb.qc.ca/eng/; **e-mail:** auberge@ssadb.qc.ca

Accommodations: Houses up to 107 guests in single, double, and triple rooms, each with private bath. Dormitories are also available.

Meals: Three meals daily in cafeteria

Costs: Rates are for room only. Single occupancy is $44, double occupancy is $58, and triple occupancy is $73. Accommodations in dormitory are $21.45 per person per night.

Directions: From points west, take Autoroute 40 East. Stay on 40, following signs to Sainte-Anne-de-Beaupré. Autoroute 40 East ends at Autoroute 138 East, becoming 138. Stay on 138 until you arrive at Sainte-Anne-de-Beaupré. Turn left on rue Regina.

Public Transportation: There is air, train, and bus service to Quebec City. Contact reception staff for complete information.

History: The auberge is a ministry for those visiting the Shrine of Sainte-Anne-de-Beaupré. Founded in 1658, there has been a shrine on this site for more than 350 years. During construction of the first church, one of the construction workers was miraculously cured of lumbago. The shrine attracted ever-increasing numbers of pilgrims, and subsequent churches were built in 1661, 1676, and 1876. The present basilica dates to 1923 and attracts a half million visitors annually.

Description: The shrine basilica is a massive Romanesque-style stone church. On the façade, between the twin spires, there is a gilded statue of Saint Anne, mother of the Virgin Mary. Visit the hillside behind the church to see its Stations of the Cross. Nearby is the Scala Sancta, a re-creation of the Holy Stairs climbed by Jesus to meet Pontius Pilate on the eve of the Crucifixion. The shrine museum has permanent installations regarding Saint Anne, the history of the shrine, and religious art.

Points of Interest: West of Sainte-Anne-de-Beaupré and farther down the St. Lawrence River are the spectacular Montmorency Falls and Quebec City, which is picturesque and charming.

Les Recluses Missionaires

12050 E. Gouin Blvd., Montreal, QC H1C 1B8

Order: Les Recluses Missionaries (Roman Catholic)

Contact: Guest Mistress

Telephone: 514-648-6801. Best times to call: 8 AM to 11 AM and noon to 4:30 PM Eastern Time

Web site: www.reclusesmiss.org; **e-mail:** hotellerie_mtl@hotmail.com

Accommodations: Monastery accommodates up to 12 guests, in eight single and two twin-bedded rooms, two of which have private baths. Additionally, there are hermitages, each with kitchenette, toilet, and shower.

Meals: Three "ordinary, healthy, and complete meals" daily

Costs: Suggested donation of $50 per day for room and meals, single occupancy, $55 per day for room and meals, double occupancy, and $55 per day for hermitages.

Directions: The monastery is located at the far east end of the island of Montreal. Take Autoroute 40 Métropolitaine. Exit at Blvd. St-Jean-Baptist North (Exit 83 driving west; Exit 85 driving east). Proceed to Gouin Blvd. Turn right; monastery is 2 kilometers (1.25 miles) down boulevard.

Public Transportation: Take Montreal Metro (subway) to Henri-Bourassa station. Then take city bus #49 (Maurice-Duplessis) to corner of Perras and Blvd. St-Jean Baptist, then bus #183 (Gouin) to monastery. Alternately, take subway to Honoré-Beaugrand station, then bus #186 (Sherbrooke) to corner of Gouin Blvd. and Sherbrooke St. Then take bus #183 (Gouin) to monastery. From Montreal Dorval Airport, take airport bus to subway (Berri-UQAM station) and then to one of the stations as above. If arriving in Montreal by train, from the Gare Centrale take subway to one of the stations above.

History: To some extent both Montreal and Les Recluses Missionaires share the same roots and history. In 1535 the French explorer Jacques Cartier visited the Indian village of Hochelega, climbed to the mountaintop, and proclaimed it *un mont real* (a royal mountain). During the century following, French men and women settled at Ville Marie near the same site, not to trade, but to work as missionaries among the Indian population. One of the women, Jeanne LeBer, wishing to devote her life to prayer and solitude, lived as a hermit, first in a house and later in a wing attached to a convent chapel. Living in solitude for 34 years, she died in 1714. More than two centuries later, in 1942, three women, inspired by Jeanne LeBer, lived in seclusion and poverty and founded Les Recluses Missionaires. The Montreal monastery was opened in 1950 along the Rivière des Prairies and today is home to 30 sisters.

Points of Interest: Since Montreal and Ville Marie were founded as a sacred city, there are many places of historic and religious interest in the area. The Notre-Dame-de-Bon-Secours Chapel was built in 1771. The city's cathedrals include Notre-Dame Basilica (1829) in the Old City, Mary Queen of the World Cathedral (built in 1855 as a one-quarter-scale replica of St. Peter's Basilica in Rome), and the Anglican Christ Church Cathedral (English Gothic Revival style, built in 1857). The largest and most visited of the churches is St. Joseph's Oratory. Rising more than 850 feet above sea level, the Oratory's huge dome dominates the city's skyline.

Special Note: The sisters offer "accommodations in the guest facilities of the monastery for anyone seeking a propitious place to meet the Lord in prayer, silence, and peace."

> *Par Lui,*
> *Avec Lui,*
> *En Lui.*
>
> *Through Him,*
> *With Him,*
> *In Him.*
>
> —RECLUSE SISTERS' MOTTO

Monastère Notre-Dame de Mistassini

100 Route des Trappistes, Dolbeau-Mistassini, QC G8L 5E5

Order: Cistercian (Trappist) Monks (Roman Catholic)

Contact: Père Hôtelier (Guest Master)

Telephone: 418-276-0491. **Best time to call:** 9 AM to 11 AM or 2 PM to 5 PM Eastern Time

Web site: www.monasteremistassini.org; **e-mail:** hotelier@monastere mistassini.org

Accommodations: Guest section of monastery accommodates 17 individuals, in 11 single and three twin-bedded rooms, each with private bath.

Meals: Three meals daily

Costs: "Your generosity."

Directions: From Quebec City take Route 175 North to Route 169. Continue north on Route 169 around Lac Saint Jean to Dolbeau.

Public Transportation: There is bus service from Quebec City to Dolbeau, and taxi service from Dolbeau to monastery. Call Taxi Léo Cadoret in Dolbeau (418-276-3136) or Taxi Centreville in Mistassini (418-276-1533).

History: The monastery was begun in 1892 and became an independent abbey in 1935. The monks support themselves by making confections in the Chocolaterie. The chocolates are for sale at the monastery and on-line.

✤ SASKATCHEWAN

St. Peter's Abbey

Box 10, Muenster, SK S0K 2Y0

Order: Benedictine Monks (Roman Catholic)

Contact: Guest Master

Telephone: 306-682-1775

Web site: www.stpetersabbey.ca; **e-mail:** guestmaster@stpeters.sk.ca

Accommodations: Severin Hall guest wing houses up to 30 individuals. There are 15 twin rooms, eight with private baths and seven with sinks.

Meals: Three meals daily

Costs: $35 per day for room and meals, single occupancy, and $45 for twin

Directions: The abbey is 70 miles east of Saskatoon on Highway 5.

Public Transportation: The Saskatchewan Transportation Company (STC) has bus service from Saskatoon and Regina to Muenster. Contact the guest master for further information.

History: Monks were among the first settlers in the area, arriving in 1903 to provide pastoral care to the German pioneers at St. Peter's Colony. Printing (German language) and farming were also some of the first works of the monks here. St. Peter's College was opened in 1921, and a new guest wing (Severin Hall) was completed in 1976. The present church was built in 1991.

Description: The church, Severin Hall, the monastery, and the college are a connecting complex of buildings. The extensive property includes woods with trails. The open areas encompass farmland, grain fields, orchards, gardens, and parks.

Point of Interest: St. Peter's Cathedral, which has murals painted in 1919 by the German artist Berthold Imhoff, is 1 mile north of the abbey.

Special Note: "Guests are invited to share our food, work, and prayer."